12-3-92

Christopher de Dios,

* Pistas Allegrias!

Minturn de Dios

* Happy Trails

INDIAN HUNTS AND INDIAN HUNTERS
OF THE OLD WEST

INDIAN HUNTS AND INDIAN HUNTERS OF THE OLD WEST

Dr. Frank C. Hibben

Illustrated with authentic photographs
from the author's files

SAFARI PRESS
(A Division of The Woodbine Publishing Co.)

P.O. Box 3095, Long Beach, CA 90803, USA.

Hibben, Dr. Frank C.

Outdoor Life Book Club imprint

ISBN 0-940143-43-7

1992, Long Beach, California

10 9 8 7 6 5 4 3 2 1

Readers wishing to receive the Safari Press catalog featuring many fine books on hunting big game all over the world should write to: Safari Press, P.O. Box 3095, Long Beach, CA 90803.

Dedication

To my old friends of the lion trail—Home Pickens, Frank Colcord, the Lee brothers (especially Dale and Clell Lee), Cass Goodner and Orville Fletcher; and to my Indian friends especially Juan de Dios, Tony Medina, Santiago Chiwewe and to a host of others who are safe with the Cloud People in the sky—to all of them, this book is affectionately dedicated.

Acknowledgement

The author and the publisher would like to thank the University of New Mexico for their kind cooperation in making available many of the pictures shown in this book.

TABLE OF CONTENTS

FOREWORD

One of the very first books I remember reading in English (I was born in the Netherlands) was Dr. Frank Hibben's HUNTING IN AFRICA. That copy came from the library of my late uncle who was a great naturalist and spent many years of his life studying the wildlife of Ethiopia. Later, when I came to the United States to study at the University of Southern California, I took the very first opportunity to read some of Dr. Hibben's other great books, namely HUNTING AMERICAN BEARS and HUNTING AMERICAN LIONS. All of his books kept me reading until very late at night.

It will, therefore, not be hard to imagine my joy when I learned that Dr. Hibben had written a new book and was looking for a publisher. In his latest book, INDIAN HUNTS AND INDIAN HUNTERS OF THE OLD WEST, you will find yourself caught up in the author's adventures in the Southwest when life was a lot more rough and tumble than it is today. But you will also find in between the covers of this book exciting true-life stories as told to Dr. Hibben by Juan de Dios, a Navajo by birth whose personal history chronicles and mirrors the very essence of the Old West. Dr. Hibben's recreation of the tales told to him include some very interesting outdoor stories as well as some frontier history never before documented. Whether you will read this book in one long drawn-out session or savor it in short snatches, you will find yourself drawn into the action by an author whose stories are a joy to read.

The Publisher
Long Beach, California
September 1989

JUAN DE DIOS

CHAPTER I

T he life of Juan de Dios is a story of many people and many places. I first met Juan in 1933 when he was leader of a group of Indians and cowboys eking out a living in the depression period by hunting wild horses along the Chama River of New Mexico. I also traveled with Juan over the Indian trails of the region and camped with him at places where the Apaches and Utes camped not so long ago.

Juan de Dios was a Navajo Indian by birth. He was captured in a slave raid and brought back to Abiquiu, New Mexico. At Abiquiu, the original territorial capital of the New Mexican region, Juan became the property of the Gonzales family. He was treated kindly and taught to handle horses and punch cattle. From his masters he learned to speak Castilian Spanish. More important, perhaps, for his later life, Juan became acquainted with several groups of Jicarilla Apache Indians and some Utes who came into Abiquiu after the United State government had established a ration point there to issue food and supplies to the Indians.

Juan believed he was twenty-one years old when Lincoln's Emancipation Proclamation freed all the slaves, Indian as well as Negro. At the time I knew him, he certainly was over ninety, yet he rode a horse like a young vaquero and his eye was as keen as it must have been in the days after the Civil War.

As Juan never knew his real name, he called himself Juan de Dios (John of God). Because he had been associated with a famous New Mexican family, he enjoyed a certain status in the troubled times following the Civil War. He was allowed to carry a gun and to come into Abiquiu and Santa Fe, privileges that were denied to most other Indians.

But by choice, Juan lived and camped with the Jicarilla Apaches.

He was a part of the exciting times when the great wagon trains came down over the Santa Fe Trail. Juan hunted buffalo and antelope and sold the dried meat to the incoming Americans. When the occasion seemed to demand, he joined in attacks on those same wagon trains. The massacre that took place at Medio Dia must have occurred about 1870. Juan told me the story when we were camping one night in the same area.

The other accounts tell of the doings of Juan de Dios and his friends. There are stories, too, of other chiefs of the Pueblo tribes along the Rio Grande. These pueblo people, although principally farmers, were hunters in their own right. Each pueblo has a hunting society with its own hunting kiva as a meeting place. My friend Cass Goodner and I knew many Indians as close friends. Through Juan de Dios, we met several of the greatest Indian hunters of the Chama and Rio Grande areas. Juan's cabin and corrals were at Abiquiu on the Chama River. There such chiefs as Tony Medina of Zia Pueblo, Sicily Atole of the Jicarilla Apaches, and Santiago Yepa of Jemez Pueblo came to pay their respects to Juan or to join in the wild horse hunts that Juan organized. We also came to know their ways. Outsiders who occasionally went with us on these later hunts thought the Indian ideas quaint and strange. Cass Goodner and I know better. We also have a great respect for bears and lions and have come to know their powerful medicine.

MASSACRE AT MEDIO DIA

CHAPTER II

A t the first scattered volley of shots, the near horse of the lead team dropped in the traces. The two bearded men on the wagon seat crumpled forward and fell beneath the wheels, and the wagon bounced over them. The remaining horse circled wildly, dragging its dead teammate in the harness. The wagon tongue caught on a projecting sod and bent upward in the middle like a folding knife. As it fell over sideways, a horse screamed. Spurts of flour rose like white smoke from the burst barrels in the wagon bed.

As the powder cloud from the first shooting drifted away, the other wagons galloped frantically past the wreck of the first one. Cotton puffs of smoke came from the tailgates as the teamsters returned the fire. All the Indians jumped on their horses, which two Utes were holding behind the ridge. The nondescript band mounted in confusion and rode down on the fleeing wagon train in scattered groups. A single Indian in full buckskin and with a round Spanish sombrero on his head seemed to be the leader, although he did not ride in the forefront of the attackers.

The wagon train had come down the grade from Raton Pass when it was fifty-five days out from Independence, Missouri. The horses were thin and the men long-bearded. It was a dry fall; the dust was thick on the trail. The yellowed leaves of the mountain cottonwoods at the foot of Raton Mountain were frosted with white dust. The men driving the wagons were-ashen faced and their eyes were ringed with red.

These men were in a black mood because they had paid a toll of gold pieces at Raton Pass. Every wagon paid Uncle Dick Wooton $1.50 to cross the tollgate at the crest of the road. The loss of these gold pieces, counted out into Wooton's callused hand, would cut their profit from the journey still further.

3

A day's travel below Raton Pass, the wagons passed through the bottoms of Vermejo Creek. Between the head of Vermejo and the Canadian was a Jicarilla Apache and Ute camp. The Indians' houses were tipis of buffalo hide and wickiups made of piñon logs and dirt. The Indians themselves were a mixed lot, underfed and poorly clothed in such fragments of castoff buckskins and trade goods as they could beg or steal from the wagon trains that passed that way. A few of the Apaches halfheartedly tried to sell dried buffalo meat to those wagoners who needed supplies. But most of the Indians and their women just stared dull-eyed at the lines of wagons that came down the trail from the pass. The Indian dogs barked and put their tails between their thin hindquarters when the oxhide whips of the teamsters cracked over the backs of the horses and wagon brakes screamed as the heavily loaded vehicles came down the grade into the creek bottom.

In this particular group of wagons, there were only nine vehicles, with twelve men riding on the wagon seats or sitting their tired horses that followed behind. The whole wagon train apparently belonged to a tall, redheaded fellow who sat carelessly on a roan gelding in front of the lead team. The man's narrow face was mottled white and brown like the skin of a piebald horse, and his front teeth stuck out like a beaver's. This man laughed as though he were glad to be across Raton Pass and onto the last stretch of road to old Santa Fe with no dangers before him. The rest of the wagoners glumly thought of the Indians they had seen before and eyed the dirty Apaches with hatred and suspicion. They had been attacked by the South Cheyennes at Timpas Creek, south of Bent's Fort, and in the running fight that followed, they had lost one wagon and three horses.

In the lead wagon, too, was a blue-eyed woman, who sat apart on her end of the wagon box and clung tightly with one hand to the iron rail there as the vehicle jolted and lurched over the last of the rough trail. Although she must have come some six hundred fifty miles already on the Santa Fe road, she was dressed as though for a city street in Chicago and showed no familiarity with either the lurching wagon or the teamster who drove it. The woman was young, about twenty-five, and she wore a red dress with some kind of little apron in front. She was bareheaded, with honey-colored hair that was powdered with dust like frost on flower. Her skin in its whiteness was curiously different from that of the sunburned and bearded men of the rest of the train.

As the wagons bunched and stopped before the Indian encampment, the men eased the brakes from the wagon tires and rested the horses. The woman in the red dress continued to look straight ahead as the silent Apaches and Utes crowded around. She acted like royalty in a hostile country, and she did not answer when one of the teamsters asked her with rough humor if she wanted him to lift her down. The woman shrank away visibly when two of the Apache squaws, with dark red strings of fly-covered buffalo meat in their grimy fingers, pressed the repulsive stuff toward her. She acted as though she thought the Indian women were reaching to drag her down with their filthy hands. Fortunately, a dogfight diverted the Apaches at that moment, when one of their bone-thin curs, with a rare show of audacity, snatched a piece of the buffalo jerky and ran under a wagon with the prize. The rest of the dogs pursued in an angry snapping melee. The noise started even the tired team horses to pitching in the harness. Driving the Indians back with curses, the wagoners climbed again on the wagon seats. Whips snaked out over the rumps of the paired teams and snapped puffs of dust from dirty hides as the wagons once again creaked into motion.

That night, the men and the strange woman, as aloof as ever, camped on the bank of Vermejo Creek, an hour's ride from the Apache camp. Here there was no danger from Cheyennes or Kiowas. They were safely through the usual hazards of the Santa Fe

Trail. In another five days, even with slow going, their wagons with cargoes of trade goods would be safe in the Santa Fe plaza. It was for this reason, perhaps, that the red-haired man with the piebald face rolled out a wooden keg of whiskey and knocked in the head with the butt of his hatchet. The other men dipped cups into the broken barrelhead and ladled out the pale red stuff to pour down their dust-caked throats. Before dark, most of the men of the wagon train were laughing hilariously, and some of them, very drunk, lay breathing heavily beside the wagons where they had fallen.

As darkness came, someone lighted a fire and the men finished the keg of whiskey there by the dancing flames. The redheaded man and two or three others looked toward the woman in the red dress, their eyes bright with the whiskey they had drunk. They plainly thought it only right that the honey-haired woman should celebrate with them the safe passage of the Santa Fe Trail.

But as on many a night before when they had attempted familiarities, she held the rough men at bay by her coldness. They suspected, too, that she carried a small pistol in the folds of her skirt, for she always held one hand concealed there. Though whether she would turn the weapon on any man who approached her or upon herself, they did not know.

So it was that four of the teamsters, with the mottled-faced one at their head, started back on foot toward the Apache encampment. The whiskey within them made the Indian women seem less dirty and repulsive than they had appeared that same afternoon. And then, there was a certain Apache girl of perhaps sixteen years who had seemed cleaner than the rest and might be friendly.

The dogs barked as the men came among the tipis and wickiups. A few Indians looked out through the doorways and then shrank back. The teamsters pounced with howls of laughter upon one woman and then threw her aside and kicked her when they saw she was old. They caught another girl, who was fleeing from one

6

wickiup to another. Perhaps this was the one they remembered. It was then that one of the Utes, an old man with bent shoulders, came before the teamsters. He held up his hands for them to stop. Perhaps they did not see him in the darkness or notice that he held no weapon. The redheaded man shot the old Ute with a .44 pistol that he jerked out of his belt. He pushed the limp body to one side with his foot with as little compunction as he would have shown in spurning the coils of a rattlesnake he had just killed.

Other Apaches and Utes came out of their lodges at the sound of the shot. An ineffectual arrow or two whistled through the darkness and thudded to the hard trampled ground beyond. Another gun banged. Shouts arose and the dogs barked louder. The teamsters began to retreat, firing as they went. Another Apache who appeared dimly before them threw up his hands and fell backwards as a heavy bullet spun him halfway around. In the noise and confusion, the white men gained the edge of the encampment and the bushes along the creek and walked single file back to their wagons. They still laughed softly among themselves as they looked backward for signs of pursuit, but the effects of the whiskey had died within them.

In the Apache camp behind them, there was an angry stir and the murmur of guttural voices. The bodies of the three dead men had been brought to the center of the encampment and laid out for the women to mourn over. The rest of the men gathered to one side. A single figure was in their midst. This man seemed taller than the Apaches and Utes and heavier in build, although he, too, was an Indian. Even as they spoke to the man in Apache, they addressed him by the Spanish name of Juan de Dios. "Juan of God" was not unknown on the Santa Fe Trail. Any Indian, and any white teamster, for that matter, had heard of the Navajo plainsman. There was perhaps no man in the whole territory of New Mexico who could hunt better, shoot straighter, or follow the obscure mountain trails more unerringly than Juan de Dios. It was natural that the Apaches should want him to lead them.

So it was decided there in the darkness, with the ululations of the Apache women in the background, that the wagon train would be destroyed. The red-haired white man with the beaver teeth would be killed and all his people with him. Every warrior in the group claimed the beaver-toothed one as his own special victim.

This was not the first time that this particular band of Apaches had planned to attack a wagon train, nor was it the first such escapade for Juan de Dios, but none of these renegades would have planned such a raid between Raton and Santa Fe. Fort Union lay only two days' ride to the south. In the fall of the year, the wagon trains were scarcely out of sight of each other on that stretch of train, and there was U.S. cavalry at Fort Marcy, near Santa Fe itself. But in the excitement of revenge and with the weapons brandished there as the crowd shouted for killing, no one thought of caution. Curiously, there was little talk of the rich plunder they might get from the wagons.

That same night, some thirty of the Apaches mounted an assortment of horses and rode away into the darkness. A New Mexico-born wastrel named Rubio, "The Blond One," rode with them, although his motives must have been different from their own. There were also two or three Utes and a Taos outcast called Beaver Itch. Juan de Dios, on a white mare, led the motley column due south in the darkness. Most of the Apaches wanted to attack the redheaded one's wagon train at dawn while the teamsters were still sleeping off the liquor. But Juan de Dios knew that this was impossible so close to the other wagon encampments. So the Indians followed him blindly across the creek bottom and onto the rolling flats on the other side. The hooves of their horses could follow the deep-cut wagon ruts of the trail, though the night was moonless and thunder muttered from scattered clouds around the horizon.

Some of the Apaches carried muskets, old-fashioned guns and no match for the new Sharps and repeating rifles that some of the wagoners brought from St. Louis and Independence. Most of the Indians were armed with bows that shot metal-tipped arrows. These iron arrowheads they had found along the Santa Fe Trail. At close range, a man could shoot such an arrow clear through the body of a buffalo so that the shaft would drop out the far side. For close fighting, such a bow and arrow is better than a gun, but how could they get so close?

A half-day's riding south of the Vermejo bottoms lies a gentle swale with a marshy spring at its center. This place is called Medio Dia because the teamsters often stopped there at midday to water their horses. It was the custom among the freighters on the Santa Fe Trail to start their wagons early in the morning without feeding either horses or men. Then, when they had traveled some ten or twelve miles, they stopped for a meal. It was at this time that the horses were most tired and the men least vigilant.

Juan de Dios knew these things well, for he had traveled with the trains both as guide and as hunter. Some of the Apaches who knew Juan de Dios the least complained bitterly at riding so far. They wanted to turn and attack the wagons of the redheaded one as soon as he drew away from his camping place. But Juan de Dios restrained them. If the point riders of the other wagon trains heard the firing, they could catch the Apaches from behind. Medio Dia was far enough from the camping places along the Vermejo and the Canadian and yet not too close to Fort Union, which was the next place where a cavalry patrol might interfere with their plans.

By the time the poorly assorted cavalcade had reached Medio Dia, it was late in the morning. The wagon wheels of the last groups that had passed through the day before had bitten deeply into the soggy ground that spread out below the spring. There was the litter of people who had passed that way—fragments of clothes, shattered

9

bottles, and a broken bedstead that somehow had gotten so far on the trail but had not stayed together to reach Santa Fe. But nowhere in the expanse of the gentle sloping valley was there any human being or any sign that human beings had been there within the last few hours.

Alongside the Medio Dia spring, perhaps a hundred yards away, was a low ridge with an outcrop of dirty brown sandstone sticking out of its crest like bones protruding from the eroding skeleton of a long-dead carcass. Cautioning the Apaches against leaving fresh tracks in the marshy ground, although in any event it was unlikely that the teamsters would notice them among so many other imprints, Juan led the horsemen along the hard ground below the low ridge and behind it. It would make an ideal ambush.

The courage of most of the Jicarilla Apaches had ebbed during the long ride. They muttered among themselves. Some wanted to ride back to their women. Others complained that they should have attacked under cover of darkness. Picking out the one man whom he knew best, Apache Charlie, a bandleader and a chief, Juan sent him back up the trail to watch for the approach of any wagons and especially to report if the wagon train of the redheaded one had joined forces with any larger group.

Juan encouraged the rest of the Indians to build a fire and hold a dance to whip up their flagging spirits to the fever pitch of battle. Being an Indian himself, Juan de Dios appreciated these things. A parfleche from one of the saddles made an impromptu drum which one Apache beat with the shaft of a bow to keep time. The others shook their bows and muskets and began to shout. Red and yellow paint was taken from pouches to decorate their faces and upper bodies. These Jicarilla Apaches had hunted on the Plains and there had learned the customs of the Comanches and the Cheyennes, who taught them to "count coup"—to make a score against a dead enemy by striking the body after a kill. A warrior was known by the number of coups he had counted.

Around the fire behind the ridge at Medio Dia, many a strange coup was told of as the men worked themselves into a frenzied crescendo by shouting and dancing. There were Jicarillas there who had killed long-knife soldiers and had the brass buttons to prove it. There were others who had met the Comanches in battle and lived to tell of the encounter. There was even one who had killed a white woman within sight of the very stockade of Fort Bent and who retold, with many flourishes, the story of how he had taken her scalp and escaped across the Arkansas River that same night.

During this dancing and coup counting, Juan de Dios stood silently by himself, leaning on the muzzle of the rifle he had traded from a beaver trapper just out of Missouri. It may have been that Juan had little to tell of, although this was doubtful. Perhaps he had been long enough with the New Mexican Spaniards to think that killing and death were subjects best not spoken of. Or it might have been that this silent Navajo with the wide-spaced eyes and quiet manner was thinking of strategy and of the coming battle.

Juan de Dios seemed almost relieved when Apache Charlie pounded up on a lathered and snorting horse. "Nine wagons are coming," Charlie said in Apache as he held up his fingers to indicate the number. "And the redheaded one rides at their front as before."

Juan de Dios asked quickly if any other wagon train was in sight behind it, but the answer was drowned in a shout from the others as they shook their weapons and yelled death to the redheaded white man.

Juan de Dios himself kicked dirt over the fire. The smoke from the blaze still hung in the hollow, where there was little wind. Juan thought that the wagon train might be warned by this; but, then, white men seldom noticed such signs. Sharply, Juan cautioned the others to silence. Although the wagon train was still perhaps two miles away, there must be no sign of danger. He allocated the horses to two of the younger men, who were to hold the animals picketed well behind the ridge in a place where they could neither smell nor see the teams who drew the wagons. A whinnying horse had ruined more than one ambuscade. The other men he placed along the crest of the ridge. El Rubio, the Mexican, lay by himself at one end of the scattered line, concealed behind a clump of brown rock. The others picked their own places along the crest. Those with rifles or muskets placed them so that they could fire across the top. The bowmen needed more room and crouched on their knees, bending low so that they could rise up and fire.

It was a long wait. Juan raised his head cautiously from time to time, even before he heard the rumble of the wagons in the distance. He noticed, too, that several colored feathers showed above the rock on the crest of the ridge and two or three musket barrels protruded from among the stones. Any fool would see these signs and swing away before the trap was sprung. But it was too late now to make any changes.

In a break in the rock before him, there grew a small saltbush. Through this, Juan de Dios watched the movement at the upper end of the Medio Dia swale. There came the redheaded man on his long-legged roan gelding. He carried a rifle across his lap in the saddle. He looked from side to side as though something had frightened him, but still he came on, his horse jogging in the manner of a trailwise animal. Some distance behind came the first wagon, with two men on the wagon seat. The teamsters were silent; perhaps their drunkenness of the night before had made them so. None of the men looked to the right or the left, but all urged their teams on with occasional motions of the long reins. Perhaps they would make the noon stop here at the Medio Dia spring. If the wagons drew up before they came abreast of the little ridge, they could save themselves yet. Still, the redheaded man came on. Once, he turned in the saddle and beckoned on the lead wagon, as though he would get them through this little valley before some disaster overtook them. Now he was opposite the place where Juan de Dios lay. The curious blotched patches on the man's face were clearly visible at that distance. His mouth, too, looked evil, with the protruding teeth and a drip of brown tobacco juice that ran out of the corner of his lips and onto his dirty checkered shirt.

A rifle barrel scraped on a rock as one of the Apaches shifted his position. The ears of the roan gelding cocked at the sound, but the redheaded man did not seem to notice. Still no shot was fired.

Now the first wagon was almost opposite the Indians. The others were close behind. Back of the rock, Juan de Dios raised his hand to give the signal, but the hand never dropped in the prearranged sign for the start of the massacre. Some Apache along the line, made too eager by the dancing and shouting of the morning, touched off his musket. In another second, a ragged volley ripped out along the crest of the ridge. Arrows leaped from the taut bowstrings and downward toward the white-topped wagons. The redheaded man turned, startled, in his saddle. Horses started to run, whips cracked.

Perhaps half the guns of the Apaches had been turned toward the red-haired leader on the roan horse, but miraculously the whistling balls had passed him by. One shot tore off the brim of his hat close before his face. The roan horse went down beneath him with a broken hind leg and another shot somewhere through the animal's belly. The man stepped off easily, taking his rifle with him, and stood for a moment as though in surprise. Two or three arrows thudded around him and another buried itself in the body of the quivering horse. Certainly the man was no coward. Lifting his rifle, he fired quickly at the head of one of the attackers along the stone-crested ridge. The bullet hit the sandstone, flattened and ricocheted with the angry whine of a heavy minny ball. Only then did the redheaded man kneel behind his dead horse to reload.

As the next wagon came opposite the place where the redheaded

13

man fired across the horse, another scattered volley of shots ripped through the canvas of the wagon's top and plowed up furrows of white wood on the side of the wagon box. One of the balls collapsed an oaken rib beneath the wagon top. The white canvas cover fluttered slack and blew away. There was the blue-eyed woman still clinging to the end of the wagon seat, looking as neat and well dressed as she had when Juan de Dios had seen her at Raton Pass. She still looked straight ahead, showing no fear. It was as though she had expected this massacre.

At the sight of the woman, El Rubio, the blond-haired renegade, stood up and waved his musket. "A los caballos, amigos!" he shouted. Few of the Apaches understood any Spanish and they didn't seem to notice that this long-mustachioed, slack-mouthed white man had taken the lead from Juan de Dios. The bowmen especially had to get closer to get in their arrows. Other Apaches rushed forward on foot to circle the redheaded one.

The Indian horses were brought forward. Two mounts escaped in the confusion and ran out from behind the low ridge to gallop alongside the wagons. The other ponies reared and plunged as the Apaches ran among them. Some riders were up and away before the others could quiet their horses enough to mount.

Juan de Dios galloped over the crest of the ridge and down on the wagons. A half-dozen of the Apaches, armed with bows, detached themselves to ride down on the redheaded man, who now lay prone behind the body of the horse. As the Indians came close, he shot one clean through the chest. The other riders split and galloped around him on both sides. Leaning under the neck of his horse, in the manner of the Kiowas, an Apache shot a steel-tipped arrow into the redheaded man's back. The shaft struck just below his belt, piercing his spine. The man gave a short cry and reared up like a wounded dog. He tried to move his legs, but they trailed useless in the dirt behind him as he writhed. Even then, he turned with difficulty on one shoulder and reloaded his rifle with a brass cartridge. As he slammed down the breech of the weapon and raised it painfully to the side, the riders could see sweat on his face. His eyes were staring above his mottled cheeks and his wild red hair looked unreal. An old Apache named Dark Eyes, who had counted many coups on the Plains, rode up with his bow ready. The red-haired man shot Dark Eyes through the middle of the face, even as another arrow pierced his own shoulder. The four remaining Apaches stood their horses above his prone body and poured shaft after shaft into his back as long as he moved. His arms still twitched as he tried to reload his rifle once again. Then one of the Apaches stepped off to count coup and rip the strange red-haired scalp from his head.

Other groups of Indians had surrounded the remaining wagons. If the wagoners had drawn their teams into a tight circle, they might yet have saved themselves. But without a leader they thought only of escape. Each driver believed that he could gallop away while the Apaches engaged the other wagons. But the Indians, under the leadership of Juan de Dios, had cut off the teams within the little valley. Above the scattered sound of the firing, Juan shouted orders in guttural Apache, directing the warriors to head the wagons into the marshy ground where they could not maneuver. Indians with bows leaned from their horses to drive arrow after arrow into the sides of the plunging team animals. As the horses dropped in the traces, the wagons slowed and stopped. Teamsters fired from their wagon beds or jumped out and tried to cover themselves behind the bodies of dead or dying horses.

A few of the wagoners had picked out the imposing figure of Juan de Dios on his white mare. Heavy-caliber balls were whistling past him. Apache Charlie had been struck from his saddle at Juan's side during the first circle, but Juan himself seemed to bear a charmed life. Once or twice, he glanced over his shoulder at a long wagon

15

that had escaped south along the dry ground at the edge of the spring. Only a single man raced in pursuit. Juan could see the long wild hair and blue coat of El Rubio.

The remaining wagons of the doomed train had come to a stop. One overturned as a frantic team horse plunged in its harness. A dead man rolled out with arms and legs flopping limply as though there were no bones in his body. Another teamster stumbled from the wreck of the wagon, shot through one knee. He staggered as he tried to stand, and blood pumped in red spurts from his leg. Holding his gun in one hand, he pointed it quickly and fired as three Indians rode down on him with a wild yell. The man whirled under the heavy impact of a bullet in this throat. He turned and fell face downward, toppling across the body of his friend.

At the other wagons, the puffs of powder smoke that came from the teamsters' rifles were scattered and slackening. The Apaches did not need Juan de Dios to tell them to ride in from all sides. If a teamster was covered from one angle, he lay open to a circling horseman from the rear. Some of the younger Indians, eager to count coup as their elders had done, jumped their horses over the dead team animals, firing into the wagons as they did so.

Two other braves had dismounted and started a small fire. From this they lighted arrows, the heads of which, wound with cattail down, burned like torches. They shot these fire arrows in long arcs against the canvas top of one of the wagons where two riflemen still fired steadily. When three arrows had been implanted there, the fire spread quickly until the whole cover was a single yellow-and-red rainbow of flame. A young man jumped from the rear of the wagon, threw down his gun, and held his hands above his head as he ran forward. One of the Apaches, with a flaming arrow already on his bow, shot the young man in the side. He screamed and grasped the burning arrow in both hands as he fell forward. The other man in the wagon fired steadily from among the flames until the whole wagon box was afire. The last report from his Sharps rifle came from the middle of the fire. No Indian counted coup on his charred body.

Juan de Dios whirled his white mare to gallop after El Rubio, the white renegade, and the wagon before him. Even in the distance, Juan could make out the red spot of color that was the white woman's dress. Beside her, standing up before the jolting wagon box, the teamster was whipping his horses frantically, his arms flailing. The Mexican renegade yelled in exultation. Rising in his stirrups to level his motion, he extended his heavy musket forward along his arm. There was a spurt of smoke from its muzzle. The man ahead in the wagon arched forward as the ball struck him in the back, threw his hands up from the flying reins and dropped the oxhide whip. Like a stalk broken in the middle by the wind, he twisted and fell from the wagon.

El Rubio gave the scalping yell like any Jicarilla Apache, but he did not glance at the fallen body of the teamster. Instead, he threw away his musket and leaned forward in the saddle to spur his horse after the fleeing wagon. The frantic team horses galloped heavily in the harness, with the reins trailing in the dirt behind. Still the woman did not look backward, but clung to the wagon seat as before. El Rubio drew abreast of the jolting tailgate and then rode up alongside the woman herself. Juan de Dios was still behind, but he could see clearly El Rubio's grin as he leered at the woman across the few feet of space that separated them. Perhaps El Rubio said something which he considered appropriate.

The woman in red turned to face him. It may be that she, too, said something, although her manner seemed cool even on the jolting wagon seat, as though she were replying curtly to some braggart who had accosted her in the park. The swarthy face of El Rubio grew even darker as he drew the heavy silver-mounted pistol from beneath his belt and leveled the clumsy thing at the woman. Perhaps he only meant to scare her, for he still laughed. The woman in the red dress raised one hand from the folds of her skirt. There was a glint of morning sunlight on a shiny bit of metal at her fingertips. She seemed to point an accusing finger straight at El Rubio. There was a flat report. El Rubio still rode with his pistol extended. The woman still clung there on the wagon seat pointing with one hand at the evil man who rode so close beside her. Then the heavy pistol dropped from El Rubio's hand and was lost in the dust cloud that rose from the wagon wheels. The renegade raised his hand to his face and the red-rimmed hole there as though he were suddenly tired. His body went slack. He fell backwards out of the saddle and struck the earth heavily, to roll over and over like a dying trout thrown upon a dry bank. His horse galloped on for a while beside the wagon, then swerved away. The woman in the red dress still rode on the wagon seat with her hand outstretched, pointing to the place where the evil face had been. Juan de Dios pulled up his horse and watched as the wagon and the woman in red disappeared in a dust cloud to the south.

Later that same year, Juan de Dios heard the talk in the cantinas of Santa Fe that a woman dressed in red had driven a wagon into the plaza. The wagon, they said, was loaded with bags of gold to start a bank in New Mexico Territory.

It was during Christmas fiesta that Juan de Dios met the blue-eyed woman strolling on the plaza beneath the portico of the Governor's Palace.

She was on the arm of an American gentleman expensively clothed and wearing a beaver hat. The woman herself was dressed in red as before, but Juan de Dios would have known her had she worn any color. Their eyes met. She seemed to recognize Juan, but she said nothing. Nor did she cry out for the town constabulary, whose station was close by. That was the last time Juan de Dios saw the woman in the red dress. But in the cantinas on the back streets and around the herders' campfires, they still talk of the massacre at Medio Dia.

THE PURGATOIRE GRIZZLY

CHAPTER III

I t was a spindly tree of no great height, and its trunk was about the size of Juan's waist. As the bear stood on his hind legs, his mean little eyes were on a level with Juan's feet. Suddenly, he reached out with a curved claw, catching the sole of Juan's moccasin. The tough buffalo hide and ankle wrappings ripped away. The grizzly reached higher, swinging a big paw from the side like a drunk in a cantina fight.

Juan de Dios pulled himself further up on the slender limbs above the forks of the tree, which swayed as the grizzly clawed at the soft wood just below Juan's bare foot. Then, apparently tiring of this, the bear reached over and bit out a section of wood and bark as big as Juan's fist. Again and again he bit at the trunk just below the fork; a sharp axe could not have cut more quickly. The slender tree shivered as the bear tore out long pieces of green wood—a few more bites and it would fall.

Juan de Dios had not been hunting this grizzly. Neither he nor the dead man, Chacon, who lay by the canyon wall, had ever hunted grizzlies—or any bears, for that matter. For one thing, Apache Indians have a superstitious fear of bears. Although Juan was not an Apache, he considered himself one. After Juan was freed by the Emancipation Proclamation, he became a professional hunter, hunting mostly with the Apaches, sometimes with the Utes, sometimes with the American mountain men who were coming into the Territory to trap beaver and to trade with the Spanish settlers. The wagon trains that came by Bent's Fort on the Arkansas River and then turned south on the Santa Fe Trail needed meat, too.

Juan de Dios had a Spanish musket that he had bought on a trading trip to Mexico City. Most of the other Indians were not allowed to own firearms, but Juan was often taken for a Spaniard because he occasionally wore Spanish clothes. Mostly, though, he dressed like an Apache and hunted with Apaches in the plains country along the Arkansas and the Cimarron.

During the Civil War, which kept the white soldiers busy, times were good on the New Mexico frontier. When the war was over, many veterans came to Santa Fe and to Fort Union. Two or three wagon trains a day came down the Santa Fe Trail through Raton Pass. Game became scarce and the wagoners arrogant. When wagon drivers raped some Indian women, Juan joined with the Apaches and Utes in an attack on the wagon train. To escape a punitive force of Union soldiers, Juan and his friend Chacon, an Apache chief, fled to the breaks of the Purgatoire River, south of the Arkansas. There they hid—and hunted. It was good country. The hundreds of little, sharp-walled canyons and stone cliffs were impassable for cavalry. In the breaks, there was game and water and wood. Many elk wintered there. There were mountain sheep and mule deer and, occasionally, even a small group of buffalo.

Juan de Dios and Chacon spent the winter fairly comfortably. They built a hogan of logs and stones against the wall of a canyon near a pool of water. Both men were warmly dressed in fringed buckskin shirts and leggings made by the Apache women. They had a buffalo robe for a blanket.

Juan had two hundred rounds of caps and balls for his smoothbore musket, and Chacon owned a good bow and plenty of iron-tipped arrows, so they never lacked meat. It was a good life, though both men would have liked some cornmeal cakes and the companionship of their women. In the spring, they decided they would cross the Santa Fe Trail by night and go to get the families of Chacon's band to come and camp with them in the Purgatoire breaks.

After the snows melted, Juan de Dios and Chacon started out on their last hunt. Roaming the smaller canyons to the east was a band of bighorn sheep. Sheep were becoming scarce, though Juan could remember how common they had been when he first started to hunt in this area.

Juan and Chacon had already killed two sheep that winter; they preferred bighorn meat to any other kind. But on this spring morning, they did not reach the area where the sheep usually fed. A short distance from their hogan, the two hunters found tracks of a large bull elk that had walked on earth softened by melting snow. The hunters swung off the minutes-old track, moving cautiously around a bend in the canyon, and immediately saw the elk feeding on grass, spring-tinged with green. It was a big bull but thin and gaunt. Its antlers were chalky and almost ready to shed. Chacon nodded to Juan and the latter raised his musket and steadied it on a rock. When the elk turned broadside, Juan fired. The bull jumped violently, then galloped up the bed of the canyon, apparently unhurt. But suddenly he collapsed and died. Juan and Chacon butchered their kill on the spot, cutting out the tenderloins along the backbone. These they tied in a package of skin, which they placed in the crotch of a small tree out of reach of wolves. Still intent on a mountain sheep, they worked hard at cutting up the carcass and caching the meat high in the cottonwoods. Next day, they would pack it all back to the hogan. It was still early in the morning when they wiped their bloody hands on the grass, cleaned their hunting knives in a little pool of water, and moved on down the canyon to the breaks, where the mountain sheep usually stayed.

But the bighorns had moved. Their tracks led straight north toward the Arkansas. That evening, Juan and Chacon turned back toward their hogan, empty-handed, finding what comfort they could in the thought that they had meat, even though it was a scrawny bull elk. Just as the sun dipped behind the Spanish peaks, the two hunters turned up the little side canyon where they had left the elk meat. There were the bundles in the trees. A flock of magpies scolded in the branches above them.

Suddenly, out of the shadow of the canyon wall came a grizzly. There was a bubbling growl—and the bear was upon them. Chacon thrust out his bow and reached for an arrow behind his shoulder. The bear struck him in that instant and Chacon died without a sound. As the grizzly reached down to bite at the fallen man, Juan ran back two or three paces, cocked his musket, and fired point-blank at the bear.

As the cloud of smoke cleared, the bear charged. Juan dropped the gun and leaped for the nearest tree. He could not remember climbing it, but suddenly, he was in the forks. The grizzly reared up on his hind legs and reached for Juan's feet. A curved claw caught the sole of Juan's moccasin and ripped the whole shoe away as the hunter jerked his foot upwards. He felt a stinging pain where one claw had grooved a furrow through his flesh. When the bear took to biting pieces out of the hole, Juan could see a matted spot of bloody fur on the hump where his shot had struck. The musket ball had not even gone through the bone of the shoulder. In a few bites, the grizzly ripped away almost half of the trunk of the tree just below the crotch, and Juan could feel the tree shiver. Two or three more tearing bites and it would fall.

Juan steadied himself between two spreading limbs above the crotch, within reach of the great claws. Then, as the tree swayed dangerously, a bundle of meat swung against Juan's shoulder—the tenderloins! Holding on with one hand, Juan drew his hunting knife and cut the strip of hide that held the bundle. Then he carefully dropped it on the head of the bear. The grizzly jumped back and dropped to all fours. With a growl, he pounced on the bundle and bit it savagely, shaking it from side to side as though to kill it. Finally, the brute lay at full length on his belly and ate the meat, gulping down chunks of hide, hair and all.

Now, Juan had a chance to look around. The trees on which the front- and hindquarters of the elk were tied showed long claw marks where the grizzly had tried to reach the meat. Chacon lay where he had fallen beside the canyon wall.

"When the grizzly has fed, he will go away," thought Juan. But he did not leave, even after he had eaten the last scrap of elk skin. As dark fell, he suddenly attacked the body of Chacon, perhaps aroused by the windblown fringe on the dead man's shirt. The grizzly bit savagely at the corpse, turned it over with his claws. But he did not eat it. Then he moved beneath an overhang in the canyon wall and lay down to guard the spot. Juan removed a headband that he wore beneath his hat and tied it around his injured foot. Then he pulled his hunting shirt up around his neck against the cold night wind that blew down the canyon. By morning, he expected, the grizzly would be gone and he could come down out of the tree and reload his gun. Then he could bury the body of his friend in some cracks in the rocks, in the manner of the Apaches.

But as the long night finally gave way to dawn, Juan saw that the grizzly was still crouched beneath the overhang. The hunter was now so cramped that he would have to shift his weight. Cautiously and slowly, he put one foot, then the other, into the crotch of the tree. Now, he eased the weight on his arms and flexed them slowly. At the movement, the grizzly sprang out of the shadow and reached the tree with lightning speed. Then it reared on its hind legs and clawed at the crotch—Juan scrambled upward and jerked his feet out of the way only an instant before the hooked claws raked the wood on which he had been standing. Then the bear sank his teeth into the tree, now almost gnawed through.

One more bite—perhaps two—and the tree would fall. Juan prayed in a low voice to the Christian God of the Gonzales family and did not neglect the Apache gods of the mountains. Then a miracle happened!

The grizzly ceased its biting and stood almost motionless against the tree. His black muzzle wrinkled back and forth, smelling upward. Finally, he dropped to all fours and walked deliberately toward one of the other trees—the one in which the other bundles of meat still hung. All that day, the bear clawed futilely at the trunk. Twice it walked deliberately to the body of Chacon, growling and biting at the stiffened corpse. After the second visit, he approached the tree where Juan perched stiffly, stood erect, and rubbed his hump against that trunk—the challenge of a male grizzly toward an enemy. Juan was careful not to move, and again the bear dropped to his feet and returned to the tree where the elk meat was hung. Through the long hours of daylight, the bear traced a three-cornered path between the two trees and Chacon's body but made no further move to attack the man.

Just at dark the second day, the bear lay down again beneath the ledge to guard his meat, his prisoner, and his victim. Juan de Dios prepared to spend another night in the tree. He was beginning to feel weak and he needed water badly.

Morning dawned over the cliffs and canyons of the Purgatoire. Juan again saw the blurred outline of the bear, lying there and watching him. The Indian was certain that he could never endure another day in the tree. Even if the grizzly did not bite through the weakened trunk, Juan felt he would fall from sheer weakness and lack of sleep. A spring wind, which freshened with the coming of the morning, swayed the tree dangerously. If the wind grew stronger, the spindly trunk would buckle. That would be the end.

Late that morning, the grizzly emerged and looked upward at Juan with bloodshot little eyes. "Now he will push against the tree," Juan thought. "In a little while, I will be again with Chacon." But the grizzly wrinkled his nose, turned, and lurched down the canyon. Once, it stopped and looked back. Then it was gone around the curve of the rock.

It might be a trick to lure him out of the tree, but Juan did not care. He fell to the ground. His numbed legs would not hold his weight, so he crawled to where his musket lay. Sitting there, he reloaded the musket and put a cap on the nipple.

It was a day later that Juan came back to the little canyon to bury his friend Chacon. The grizzly had not returned, but Juan did not track it, nor did he retrieve the elk meat from the other trees. There would be no refuge for the Apache family in the Purgatoire canyons. No Indian would ever hunt there again. The big grizzly was evil medicine.

DEAD MAN'S STAMPEDE

CHAPTER IV

T he roar of hooves on the hard ground was a thundering rumble of sound. All the hunters raised their heads. They thrust their weapons above the edge of the cutbank of the arroyo. Less than an arrowshot away, the dark line of the herd swept past in a confused mass of galloping forms. Each man picked out a cow or a young bull on the edge of the jostling animals. Dust, boiling up from the thousands of hooves, eddied in yellow clouds back and forth with the changing wind. Off to the right, a shot boomed out. At the sharp sound, the rumble of hooves increased. Each animal broke into a hacking run.

Juan de Dios rested his musket on the edge of the cutbank and picked out a fat cow. The dust clouds swirled away like smoke from a forest fire. There was his animal! He settled his sights on the cow's shoulder, well below the hump. He noticed the cow held her muzzle high, feeling for the wind. Other buffalo, through the dust clouds, seemed painted on a dirty canvas. The edge of the herd milled and turned together. Again the gun on the right blasted. The lead bulls swung their forequarters and ran toward the arroyo.

"That cursed Chino," Juan muttered under his breath, "and that antelope!"

As the buffalo swung together, Juan lost sight of his fat cow. There she was again! Her head moved up and down as she ran. There were moving heads and humps on all sides. Out of the billows of dust charged a solid wall of galloping buffalo. They were coming straight at the line of hunters behind the cutbank. Juan swung his musket to cover the shoulder of the nearest bull. He jerked the trigger. The sound of the shot was drowned out by the thunder of noise from the buffalo. He could not see whether his animal went down or not. The gap was swallowed instantly by a hundred other buffalo galloping out of the dust. Juan could see the protruding tongues and glaring eyes of the buffalo in the lead. He could hear the grunting roars of the foremost bulls. He dropped down with his back to the cutbank and began to reload frantically.

"That cursed Chino and his antelope!"

Juan de Dios and Chino had been friends for many years. Chino was an Jicarilla Apache chief and perhaps the best hunter of all the northern Apaches. Juan de Dios himself was not an Apache, although he considered himself one. He had been born a Navajo, and he had been told, when he was old enough to be interested in such things, that he had been captured as a baby in a slaving raid by a group from Santa Fe and sold to the Gonzales family of Abiquiu in New Mexico Territory. Juan later called himself Juan de Dios, or "John of God," as a gesture toward his owners and benefactors, the Gonzales family.

At this time, when Juan was a young man, the U.S. government, attempting to pacify the Indians of the Southwest and to keep them from raiding settlements and wagon trains on the Santa Fe Trail, gathered the various tribes together on reservations and fed them at ration points to keep them under control. Abiquiu was one of the ration points for the Jicarilla Apaches. Juan de Dios camped with the Apaches, learned to speak their language, and later married an Apache woman. It was at this time, too, that Juan came to know Chino, an Apache chief who was not satisfied to eat the white man's beef. Chino much preferred his own meat, and he liked the wild, unfettered life that went with it.

Following the Civil War, times were difficult in the Territory of New Mexico. Wagon trains coming down the trail from Fort Bent killed or scared away most of the game. The soldiers from Fort Union were even worse. Each day, the garrison sent out scouting and hunting parties. Buffalo and most of the other game disappeared within two days' ride of Fort Union or the Santa Fe Trail.

Chino and Juan de Dios made some concessions to the changing times by hunting meat in such areas as they could find game. This meat their women dried. The jerky they sold to the wagoners along the trail, who often did not have time to hunt themselves. At one such contact, Chino acquired a cap-and-ball musket, although there was some question as to whether Chino got the gun by trade or by stealing. Juan de Dios owned a smooth-bore musket of Spanish manufacture, which he had bought in Old Mexico some years before. Because the U.S. Army was trying to keep firearms from falling into the hands of Apaches, it was especially imperative that Juan and Chino keep out of sight of army patrols when carrying guns. For this reason and also to get away from the dangerous and gameless terrain near Fort Union, they crossed the Santa Fe Trail by night and moved down the Cimarron River toward Point of Rocks. About thirty other Apaches traveled with the two. Some of these were Chino's immediate family, with a number of extra women who would be handy to skin game, jerk meat, and get wood and water. There were others, too, dissidents who wanted to get away from ration points and a few renegades already in trouble who had to escape the long arm of the U.S. Cavalry. About half of the ill-assorted group were not mounted, and only three of the men in addition to Chino and Juan carried guns. Chino chafed at the delay caused by the walking women. Such horses as they had, of course, the men rode. Also, such a large band left a broad trail in their wake, which any cavalry patrol could quickly follow. But there was no help for it, so Juan and Chino pressed on to the east of Point of Rocks with long night marches. Four days east of the Santa Fe Trail, the party turned south along the edge of the Staked Plains. Here they could get wood and water from the springs that seeped beneath the rimrocks. Just to the east below the Staked Plains were the buffalo prairies. Ten years ago, at the time of the Great War, from camp on the rimrocks the hunters might have seen herds of buffalo as far as the eye could reach. Now as they made camp, there was nothing, or almost nothing. Three antelope were the only living things in the distance. Too many war parties and too many hunters had passed this way. The days of buffalo hunting were almost over.

Chino eyed the three antelope as the women slowly began to unload the tipis and make camp below the rimrocks in a group of juniper trees. An antelope represents little meat, especially for thirty people, but Chino needed an antelope hide. Antelope skin is the major item used in an Apache ceremony held to foretell the future. Chino wanted to hold such a ceremony to see what the will of the gods might be. With blue-coated soldiers taking over the territory, with the buffalo almost gone and the Apache captive on reservations, the future seemed dark and uncertain. To see what each future year will bring, the Apaches hold an animal relay race, with one side representing meat and the other side representing vegetable food. Whichever side wins indicates what kind of food the Apaches will have in the future. If the race is a draw, starvation wins.

Chino set out alone to try to shoot one of the three antelope so that the ceremony could be held. But hunters' luck is always uncertain. The antelope were in the open prairie with no cover close. Chino crawled up a shallow draw to try to get within range of the closest antelope. In the draw lay a lone buffalo bull, gaunt and old. The bull stood up and stared at the crawling human. Chino rose to his knees and shot the bull through the heart. The three antelope ran off. Chino walked back to get the women to cut what meat the could from the emaciated buffalo.

Scrawny buffalo meat, and that from only one animal, is poor food for thirty people. In spite of this, Chino insisted that the ritual relay race be run so that they would all know what the gods would tell. The fresh buffalo skin was used instead of the traditional antelope skin, but perhaps in these difficult times the gods would not mind.

Six men were chosen for each side—one to represent the meat world and the other the vegetable kingdom—and the race began. All the runners were tired and hungry, but the six meat runners came in first by a wide margin.

Chino shook his head and looked out again over the prairies to the east. How could the Apache have meat? There was no game. Even the three antelope had disappeared. Juan, who had spent most of his life in the town of Abiquiu, did not place such great confidence in Apache gods. He thought that all of Chino's band might well starve to death with shriveled bellies before they found enough food, either meat or vegetable.

Chino, because of the prophecy, urged that the band move two days' march out into the prairie. Yet he was uncertain whether the prophecy was correct, because a buffalo skin had been used instead of an antelope skin. Juan, and most of the others, thought a move to the east was the height of folly. They would probably find little meat, but they almost certainly would find a war party of Comanches or Kiowas. At Juan's urging, they compromised on a day's march to the southwest along the rimrocks, where they could find some shelter.

In the evening, they camped in a swale where a wide, sandy wash called Ute Creek cut through the edge of the Staked Plains. In the dry bed of the creek at one place was a perennial pool of muddy water. Juan had camped at the spot once before. Ironically, it was called Buffalo Springs.

Just beyond the creek bed, a small mesa stands alone as a last remnant of the Staked Plains. Indians of long ago had built their homes and buried their dead on top of this mesa. The Apaches had long called the spot Place of the Dead Man. They avoided Dead Man's Mesa and camped between the mesa and the creek so that their fires would be invisible to any enemy out on the plains. As the jaded company scattered on the poor campground, there were no tracks of buffalo or signs that any game had been there for many months.

On the next day, all able-bodied men moved out to hunt. Those with horses rode as far east into the Great Plains as their tired mounts could carry them. They came back long after dark to report that as far as they had looked, there was no fresh buffalo sign. They did find where a large war party of Kiowas had ridden south the day before, within sight of Dead Man's Mesa. Had the Kiowas seen the smoke of the cooking fires? Had they heard the shot when Chino had killed the scrawny buffalo bull?

With a war party in the vicinity, there was little chance that a buffalo herd would be in the area. Yet, if they turned back toward the Santa Fe Trail, they risked encounter with the blue-coated cavalry, and they would probably starve in any event. That night, they held a council with the council fire carefully hidden behind Dead Man's Mesa. Chino, standing by the fire, raised his face and his arms toward the edge of the mesa in the darkness and called aloud on the spirits of the dead hunters there and asked what to do. No sound came out of the darkness, but it seemed that the spirits had spoken through the relay race. Chino's band would find meat. The meat lay to the east.

The next morning at daybreak, Chino climbed to the top of Dead Man's Mesa through the break in the rock, which was the only entrance to the top. The ancients had cut handholds in the sandstone cliff and had fortified the place so that one man could hold it against an army. Chino walked with reverence among the tumbled stones of the ruined houses on top of the mesa. He stepped gingerly among the bones that eroded from the shallow earth on the crest. He looked to the east out over the rolling plains where the morning sun was just beginning to cast long shadows across the crests of the prairie swales.

There they were!

The buffalo herd was a big one—several hundred animals at least. They moved slowly up from the south on their spring migration. Some of the animals were scattered on the flanks, grazing as they walked. The whole mass moved steadily northward along the course of a dry wash.

Chino hastily climbed down through the crack in the mesa and ran to tell the others that fulfillment of the prophecy of the relay race was there to the east. He quickly organized the hunters. As the buffalo were at no great distance, they would not need the horses. At the sound of shots, the women were to bring the horses so that some mounted men could pursue the herd when the rest began to cut up the fallen animals. The buffalo were in an ideal position for an easy stalk. The hunters could go up the dry wash under cover of the cutbanks. The wind came out of the southeast with the rising sun. The gods were with them.

Chino and Juan led the knot of armed men out of the breaks at the foot of Dead Man's Mesa and toward the dry wash, perhaps a mile away. There was little chance that the buffalo would see them, but they walked crouched and in single file down the gullies and behind hummocks so that there would be no chance of alarming the herd. They reached the dry wash easily and began to move up along the curving course of the sunken arroyo. Bending low, the moving men were already close enough to hear the grunting and mumbling of the bulls on the flanks of the herd. They trotted up the winding course of the arroyo. Just ahead, the dry wash curved in a wide meander to the east, forming a sharp bank almost as high as a man's head. There the hunters would be within easy arrow-shot of the buffalo. For those with guns, it was point-blank range.

Chino pointed to the place and looked at Juan. Juan nodded his head and checked his musket. Other hunters looked to their guns. Men took arrows from their quivers. Each bowman held three arrows in his bow hand and placed one on the string. Some hunters placed additional arrows between their teeth. Chino raised his head cautiously above the level of the bank. Just opposite the huddled hunters, on the flanks of the buffalo herd, was a lone antelope buck. He was a magnificent animal. The buffalo behind were grazing and moving along. The antelope stood motionless. He was tense, with his head raised. The early morning sun glinted on his horns and on the moisture of one eye.

Chino touched the gun in his hand, pointed to the antelope, and looked at Juan. Juan shook his head vigorously. The other hunters were shuffling nervously. The buffalo moved along steadily to the north. In a few moments, they would be past the cutbanks and out of range.

Juan motioned the hunters forward. He stationed the first man where the bank of the arroyo began to curve. At intervals, the hunters stopped behind the bank with the bowmen in the middle, where the range was the closest. Juan moved to the far end of the line. He took off his old Mexican sombrero and raised his head so that his eyes just cleared the edge of the cutbank. The buffalo herd was directly abreast of the crouching hunters. As Juan calculated the situation, a faint breeze fanned his right cheek. The wind was shifting to the south. If the breeze shifted another quarter, the buffalo would wind them.

Juan looked down the line of men. Each hunter held his weapon ready and looked toward Juan. Chino was not there. Juan dropped his hand as the first signal. Each hunter raised up and extended his weapon over the edge of the cutbank. Some of the bowmen wore eagle feathers in their hair in the old manner. As the line of heads and feathers rose above the bank, the closest buffalo stopped and stared.

Juan shifted his musket to the side of a small bush and picked out a single animal. At his shot, every hunter would fire. Juan noticed out of the corner of his eye that some of the bull buffalo were milling uneasily. The wind was shifting. The animals were catching the scent of humans. Juan pressed his cheek against the stock of his musket and squinted along the sights. All the buffalo were moving now. They broke into a run. Some animals smelled humans very close. Those which had not yet caught the scent ran also. A shot boomed out. Juan had not fired. The shot had come from the right. Chino! Chino had shot that accursed antelope. From that angle, the wind blew directly from Chino to the buffalo herd.

A scattered volley of shots was almost drowned by the rumble of hooves. A few arrows arched out and fell among the dark forms of the jostling buffalo. Juan hesitated. The fat cow that he had picked out for his first shot disappeared. Billows of dust blew along the flanks of the herd. The rumble of hooves on the hard ground was deafening.

Through the dust clouds, Juan could see humps and heads moving up and down as the animals ran. Like wind in tall grass, the buffalo eddied and turned as the lead animals tried to escape from a terror they could not see. The foremost bulls swung like cavalry horses and came straight at the cutbank and the line of hunters.

As the foremost bull came out of the dust, Juan aimed at his shoulder and jerked the trigger. He did not wait to see if the animal fell. Juan dropped behind the cutbank with his back against the dirt. He began to reload frantically. Juan's musket was an old-fashioned Spanish model, which he could reload in eight seconds. This time, he bettered that mark. He slapped the cap on the nipple, swung the barrel around, and raised up.

The first buffalo were pouring over the cutbank. As he turned, Juan saw the closest men frantically firing arrows into the dark forms above them. The arrows had no more effect than sticks blown in the wind. Two men broke and ran. Crippled buffalo began to fall over the cutbank. Other animals jumped over them. A form appeared above Juan. He pulled the trigger of the musket. He felt the stock kick back along his arm. The buffalo turned in the air. The musket was kicked from Juan's hand. With a sudden thump the buffalo fell on its back in the arroyo. Juan shrank against the cutbank to escape the flailing hooves.

The dirt wall against his shoulder curved slightly inward where the torrent of the arroyo had undercut. Juan pressed into this protection, grinding his face into the dirt. All around him the earth shook as buffalo jumped or fell over him. The earth bank caved away. Juan was half-buried. A hard hoof, breaking down through the earth, struck him on the head. He remembered nothing else.

When the blackness lifted from him, Juan looked up into the face of Chino. It was a face older and more haggard by many years. As Juan raised himself on one elbow, he saw he was between a dead buffalo and the cutbank that had saved his life. Just above him lay another dead animal. But along the line where the hunters had stood, there was only pounded earth, with here and there a dead man or a hoof-trampled buffalo carcass. The stampeding animals had completely beaten down the cutbank where the men had crouched. Juan saw only one other hunter standing with Chino.

The Apaches still tell the story of the Dead Man's Stampede. Some blame the disaster on the will of the gods. Others say it was Chino's fault. Some of the old men point out the death of the hunters was read in the ceremonial relay race when a buffalo skin was used instead of an antelope hide. Everyone knows that hunting is a ceremony. The gods of the hunt are particular about the rules.

BIG MEDICINE LION
CHAPTER V

T ony Medina said nothing. Like all Indians, Tony didn't talk unless there was something to say. But Tony's dark eyes sparkled with excitement. He, too, broke into a shambling run along the edge of the cliff.

Ahead, the voices of the hound pack broke into a roar of sound. The dogs had jumped the cougar. The cry of a pack of hounds, when they're looking at a lion, would make any hunter break into a run.

Cass paused as he pressed through a thicket. "Look," he said, involuntarily. He didn't need to point to the form of the deer, lying beneath a mountain mahogany bush near the edge of the rock. The belly of the animal was half eaten away, with bloody strings of entrails trailing off into the well-trampled dirt.

"Buck," said Tony, without emotion. So it was, or had been, for the deer had four or five tines on either side of its antlers and seemed a mature and fat animal. Tony indicated a depression in the dirt with a brown finger. Cass had already seen the imprint near the neck of the deer where the ground had not been marked by the feet of the eager hounds. "It's him. That's the one!"

Cass knelt so quickly that his flat-topped sombrero fell off his head, unheeded. Even Tony seemed shaken from his usual calm. The track was that of a lion's hind foot. The circular imprint was a large as a man's hand and pressed deeply into the hard soil. The big cat had made that print only seconds before. The hounds, following the scent along the top of the cliff, had jumped the lion as he ate his first meal from the body of the buck. By the looks of the dead deer, the lion's belly must be full. Obviously, this big cougar had killed his last deer and eaten his last meal.

Cass cocked his head to one side. He said suddenly, "They're barking 'Treed.'" Tony also listened. Some of the hounds had broken into short, staccato yelps. This was the noise they made when they were looking at a quarry in a tree. Both Tony and Cass again broke into a run. The Indian's moccasined feet made no noise on the scattered rock as he passed. Cass Goodner ran with difficulty in his high-heeled boots. The dogs were just ahead, behind the few stunted pines that grew here and there along the rimrock. The sound of barking was subdued, then louder again. A questioning note seemed to creep into the noise. Some of the hounds had fallen silent.

Tony and Cass came out from behind the last tree, side by side. There were the dogs milling on the edge of the rock. There was a crack in the cliff edge here. One or two of the younger hounds tried to clamber down the precipitous rock. Then they backed up again with their feet braced. The older dogs sniffed the faint wind that came up the cliff face and barked from time to time.

"What's the matter here?" Cass said, half to himself, as he ran forward. "That lion couldn't have. . . ." Cass lay flat on his belly and craned over the edge of the rock. It was a sheer drop of sixty feet to the next ledge below. There was only one break in all of this distance. Halfway down the sandstone face was a jutting corner where a block of stone had broken away in ages past. A little dirt and a single, pathetic bush had found a purchase on this projection. Even from where he lay, Cass could see the imprint of two big lion paws on this tenuous footing. He wriggled back with difficulty and grinned a sickly grin at Tony Medina. "You'd better look at it yourself, Tony. Nobody will believe me if I tell 'em that lion jumped down the face of that cliff."

Tony Medina did not look over the cliff edge. "Big Medicine Lion. We no catch," he said laconically.

Tony had told me of a very special "Big Medicine" lion that lived in these cliffs far from Tony's native Zia Pueblo. At Zia, Tony was chief of the War Society. Members of this society are called Kimo, which means "mountain lion" in the language of the Central Rio Grande Pueblos. Members of the Kimo Society carry ancient sinew-backed bows in special ceremonies and quivers made of a cougar skin. Arrows carried in such a quiver strike like a lion and kill quickly, just as the lion does.

Long ago, before the coming of the Spaniards, the Zias had made a war shrine in the cliff canyons of the Utes, against whom they fought. The Utes raided the pueblo and stole their corn and their women. The ancient pueblo people were farmers, as are the modern Pueblo Indians, but this stealing of women was not a thing to be passed over lightly. So the Zias returned in a vengeful and punishing raid northwest into the canyon country of the Utes. It is told by the "Long Hairs" of the Zia that many Utes were killed. Many Zias were also lost and the women were not recovered. The Zia left a shrine of upturned rocks to commemorate the event and placed many prayer plumes at the site of the battle. Each year the Kimo Society of Zia makes the long trip into the Ute country, on foot, to place more prayer plumes on this sacred shrine. When Tony Medina told me of these ancient things, I wondered whether this was legend or history. Then Tony escorted me into the kiva of the Kimo Society and showed me seven scalps. Yearly, the Zias hold a ceremony and "feed" these scalps cornmeal to appease the spirits of the slain Utes.

Tony Medina told us, also, of the "Great Medicine Lion." He had seen this massive lion on the rimrocks above the ancient shrine. The big cat's muzzle was gray with age. Below his belly, a long fold of skin made a snakelike track in the snow. His tracks were splayed like those of a very old wolf. This Medicine Lion was the spirit of the Zia warriors slain in this ancient battle, Tony said,—but he left tracks in the snow between the rocks like any other lion.

As the big cat escaped, the dogs, too, seemed bitterly

disappointed. They circled in an inane fashion on the edge of the cliff. They barked and looked at the two men as though expecting these humans to do something that would save the situation. Cass looked up and down the edge of the cliff. It stretched unbroken as far as he could see in either direction. We had been following along the top of this cliff for an hour before we had jumped the lion from his kill. Long before we could retrace our steps and find some side canyon down which we could climb, the big lion would have gotten completely away.

Heedless of the danger, Cass sat down on the very edge of the rock and dangled his feet over. From time to time, he tossed little stones from the brink and measured the time that it took for them to hit the bottom. The canyon below his feet was one of many that cut in jagged black outlines through the flat-topped mesas that showed in every direction. There were other cliffs as high as or higher than the one on whose edge we sat. It was not mountainous country but an elevated plateau that had been cut into a froth of branching canyons by eroding water since the geological periods when these rocks had been lying at the bottom of some ancient sea. So straight-sided and precipitous was the area that only a hardy man would contemplate entering it at all. Because the laminated layers of sandstone, shale, and coal on the sides of these canyons looked like the leaves of a giant book to some early pioneer, this area had long ago been called the Book Cliffs.

As Cass Goodner surveyed this jumbled scene with something like hopelessness, he thought of the many disappointments that we had suffered already. Cass had hunted lions in every state in the Southwest, but he knew of no place in all of this area more rugged than the Book Cliffs of eastern Utah and western Colorado. It was here that the great deer herds that habitually feed on the western slope of the Colorado Rockies drift down to spend the winter in isolated seclusion. These thousands of deer formed a plentiful supply of meat for the lions that also called this their home. But it was the roughness of the terrain itself that was the real reason why this was ideal lion country.

"It's no wonder," Cass said meditatively, as he threw another stone off into space, "why your medicine lion lives in these Book Cliffs. Dogs and horses just can't get over this country."

Tony nodded in silent agreement. "Medicine Lion one smart lion—grow awful big," he commented.

Cass scrambled to his feet. "Tony, we've got to catch that lion." Cass emphasized his determination by throwing down a stone so that it shattered into powder on the rock at his feet. "I think that one may be a record. He has a track like a horse." Cass turned again to survey the wild canyons that surrounded us. "There's certainly nothing to keep him from growing to be the biggest lion in all creation in this mesa," Cass commented as we turned to go back to where we had left the horses in a canyon miles back along the trail.

Tony retraced his steps to the fallen buck. With a knife made from an old file, he cut away part of the haunch of the dead deer and swung it onto his shoulder. The dogs followed silently in a long line as we headed for camp.

We didn't catch the big lion of the Book Cliffs on that trip, nor did we catch him that year, although we talked a lot about it.

It had been months before when Tony Medina told us of the great Medicine Lion of the Book Cliffs. Cass decided, at that moment, to take his hound pack and try to tree the big cat. I wanted to see this mysterious cougar and photograph him and the Book Cliffs, and the place where the Zias had battled the Utes so long ago. Tony agreed to show us the sacred place, "if we do not disturb the shrine, but you will not see the Medicine Lion," he said with conviction. I noticed, as we prepared for the trip, that Tony finished painting and tying on the turkey and flicker feathers of several prayer sticks for the occasion. He put these in his battered buckskin bag.

If Cass Goodner were not a tenacious fellow, that might have ended the matter and this one famous cougar might still be guarding the Zia shrine in the canyons of eastern Utah. Instead of simply forgetting about the lion or admitting that the lion was smarter than he, Cass spent the subsequent several months in gathering equipment and making preparations for the hunt of all time. For this purpose, Cass persuaded Roy Snyder, who is a professional lion hunter for the New Mexico Department of Fish and Game, to go along on the hunt. Roy was to take a leave from his regular lion-hunting activities in New Mexico to enjoy a postman's holiday by hunting one particular lion in Utah. Both Roy and Cass were convinced that if they had two complete packs of dogs and two changes of horses for everyone concerned, the big lion could not escape them. If they couldn't outsmart him, they would simply wear him down.

It was late fall by the time we had completed all of our preparations. In addition to me, as official photographer, Cass, Tony, and Roy Snyder drove a procession of cars, jeeps, and horse trailers over the Utah roads toward the Book Cliffs. We spent three days clearing a track through an early fall of snow into the mouth of Coal Canyon, where we made a base camp. Another heavy snow over Thanksgiving weekend completely suspended hunting operations. It was two days and some hundreds of hands of poker later that we mounted our horses and took the first pack of hounds out for a hunt. That day, we caught and released a female lion.

In a natural alcove above Coal Canyon, Tony showed me the shrine. The Utes had camped there where a game trail led down through the tumbled rocks to a trickle of water in the canyon floor. The vengeful Zias had attacked from above. We found several rectangular upright stones to mark graves. There were circles of larger stones, which had held down the skirts of the Ute tipis. Roy Snyder did not laugh when Tony Medina placed three turquoise painted prayer sticks upright in a large pile of stones in the middle of the ancient encampment. The feathers on top of the prayer plumes moved in the slight wind that blew up the canyon floor. At the foot of the shrine was a broken and weathered human thigh bone and part of a whitened human skull.

During the subsequent days of the hunt, Cass and Roy alternated sets of horses and packs of hunting hounds. The deep snow and the cold were hard on both, but with a day's rest in between, the animals were fresh for each go-round. It was only the hunters who found the work exhausting. During the afternoons, the snow melted in the hot Utah sun, only to freeze and crust over during the bitterly cold nights that followed. Crusted snow, as well as the cliffs, became hunting hazards for hounds and men as well. For several days, we did not find the track of the giant male lion that we had come to see.

Roy Snyder had remarked, with his typical cowboy drawl, for the tenth time as he looked at a lion track in the snow, "That big lion of yours has kind of shrunk a little."

Tony Medina said, with spirit, "We hunt Big Medicine Lion. He got big feet—drag tail and belly in snow."

For the tenth time, also, Cass replied with some irritation, "That ain't the one. That's an ordinary lion. Tony's 'Big Medicine Lion' had big feet," as I could attest. He also had a fold of skin on his belly that left a serpentine trail between his widespread tracks in the snow.

We caught, during these experiences, several "ordinary lions." Under other circumstances, this would have been thrilling enough in itself, but this time we were not hunting ordinary lions. We were after "Big Medicine Lion." We had been riding over a week and were ten miles from base camp when we finally found it.

"Damn, Cass, that's the biggest track I ever saw. And look how he pushed down through that hard ground," Roy exclaimed.

Cass derived some satisfaction from at last showing Roy the big track. "It's old, though," Cass said by way of half-apology. "He went this way yesterday afternoon when it was melted. Shall we take it anyhow?" Cass looked at Roy.

For answer, Roy swung up into his saddle and turned his horse along the plain line of lion tracks that led toward the head of the canyon. These were not the men to quit a track even if it was twenty-four hours old and leading straight away from camp.

At that, the horsemen with their tired hounds would have had little chance of catching up to that particular cougar had it not been for one of those accidents that all hunters pray for. The hounds could not smell the track of the big lion, although Cass and Roy could see it plainly. All the scent had disappeared when the soft snow in which the cougar had planted his padded feet had frozen over the night before. Suddenly, one of the hounds that had been trailing behind pricked up her head and ran up a short side canyon, barking as she went.

"It's Sissy," said Cass disgustedly. "That whelp has smelled a porcupine."

Roy Snyder circled in the direction where Sissy had gone. He turned and grinned back over his shoulder. "Let 'er go," he yelled as he spurred his horse. "She's on the track. The big one!"

Apparently, the lion had made a great circle during the previous night and had crossed his own track low down. By that accident, the hunters had gained many hours. The new trail that Sissy had discovered had been made early that same morning. The other hounds also caught the infectious excitement and streamed past the horses at a dead run. The hunt was on!

But Cass had found before that it took more than a fresh track and a good pack of hounds to catch that particular lion. Within a mile, we caught up to the baffled dogs. The hounds were jumping toward a high ledge along the canyon wall. The big cougar of the Book Cliffs was up to his old tricks.

Cass did not waste a moment in futile chagrin. He turned his horse quickly and whistled to the dogs. At first, they were reluctant to come. Roy urged some of the laggards on with the end of his lariat. Soon the two hunters were galloping down the side canyon in the direction from which they had come. Around the next rocky headland Cass remembered a deer trail that led upward along the jagged ridge to the top of the mesa above. It was knowledge such as this that would outwit the wily cougar.

We slid off our horses before the animals came to a stop. In half an hour of heart-throbbing climbing, we topped out on the narrow mesa that flanked the canyon on that side. The older hounds of the hunting pack had already caught the spirit of the idea. In a few minutes, they streamed ahead along the mesa top. They picked up the lion track where it topped out. The old cougar had not outwitted them that time.

All hunts seem to be a succession of rising and falling hopes. So it was with this one. Roy Snyder and Cass Goodner are perhaps the two best lion hunters in the Southwest. Their hounds have many kills to their credit. But even against this competition, the big lion of the Book Cliffs was holding his own. He seemed to realize he was being followed. The track led over ledge after ledge where the dogs could not jump. Several times, the lion leaped straight upward to catch, with his giant paws, the edge of the rock in a place where no dog could go. Each time, however, the men found some way to get around these obstacles and find the track once again higher up and farther on. The chase led several miles farther back into the heart of Book Cliffs. We were now in country we did not know. Unfamiliar canyons jutted out in every direction, each one of them walled by sandstone cliffs and drop-offs that made passage impossible. It was near the head of one of these, and as darkness was falling, that we finally abandoned our horses. The hounds were still trailing steadily.

Neither man asked the obvious question, "Shall we go on?" They pulled their rifles out of their scabbards and started climbing the rocks in the direction the hounds had gone. One dog, somewhere above them, was evidently rimmed off and caught among the rocks. The long, drawn cry of the hunting hound on the trail changed to the anguished whine of a dog in trouble, but we did not deviate from our course to rescue the hound. That could come later.

By cracks and such footholds as we could find, we topped out again above the canyon. The dogs, too, had found some way to climb these obstacles, only to be blocked beyond where the lion had jumped down a cliff on the far side in characteristic fashion.

Both the hounds and the hunters seemed to realize that this was the ultimate test. If we could just pass this place—

"We no kill the Medicine Lion," Tony said, as we gathered in an indecisive group. I noticed that somehow during the chase, Tony had taken paints out of his war bag and drawn a broad band of red across the bridge of his nose and cheeks below. On each side was a streak of yellow; red is the color of blood and yellow the color of death.

Cass looked along the cliff to both sides. This sandstone cliff, like so many others in the nightmare country, seemed unbroken as far as he could see. There was just one spot that might be possible. The two men crossed to this place with the dogs at their heels. Cass looked over. No, it was suicide.

A fall of rock at some ancient time had broken away from the cliffs and poured over this place in a jumble of powdered stone and fragments. Many of these had lodged in a pile against the parent cliff. This pile was twelve or fifteen feet below the two men and a precarious footing at best. Almost in spite of himself, Cass wormed over the ledge and hung by his hands. He dropped. As his feet hit the rough rock, his legs buckled and he almost fell backwards. A short roll would carry him over another cliff below. He dropped sideways. With bleeding hands, he stopped his fall. He crouched there on the cold stone for a few moments with his muscles quivering. Then he stood up. "The guns," he said tersely.

I dropped the two rifles, one after the other. Cass caught each deftly and leaned them against the rock at his side. Then Roy and I dragged the protesting hounds by their collars to the edge of the drop-off. We held the struggling animals for a moment over the cliff edge, then dropped them into Cass's outstretched arms. Each dog licked Cass's face as he held each hound for a minute, then set him down on the rocky pile at his feet. At last, Roy and I wormed over the edge of the cliff, held by outstretched hands for an instant, then dropped. Tony jumped by himself and landed on the tumbled snowy rocks on charmed feet with the sureness of a cat.

We gathered up the rifles. The dogs were already hunting other talus piles by which they could descend other cliffs below. One of the hounds off to the left picked up the track again. The howl of the dog reverberated between the rock cliffs.

The shadows deepened into midnight blue in the canyon bottom below us. Tony Medina sang a chant low under his breath as he trotted along. Men and dogs poured down over the side of the canyon, seemingly heedless of gravity. The hounds, following the hot lion odor, went first. The trail zigzagged downward. As the foremost hounds stretched out on the canyon bottom, the dogs broke into frenzied barking. There was a clump of scraggly trees here. The shadows beneath were in almost complete darkness. The cry of the dogs became a continuous roar. Suddenly, from the gathered shadows, a darker form separated itself. Against the white snow of the canyon bottom, this form arched out in twenty-foot bounds. Beyond the trees it showed clearly.

"Look! Look!" Cass yelled and clutched me by the shoulder. "They've jumped him. That's the lion!"

The running dogs were blurred splotches against the snow as they closed with the fleeing cougar. The big cat ran easily, in graceful jumps with his long tail trailing behind. We ran down the last few yards of the canyon wall, yelling and stumbling over the rocks. When we reached the canyon bottom, our boots sank into the deep snow. We floundered and fell.

Still, the cougar ran straight down the floor of the canyon. Once, as a dog came close, the big cat turned and struck at the hound with a front paw. The rest of the dogs closed in. As the lion turned to face one dog, another hound from behind seized a mouthful of lion fur and twisted his head savagely.

Again, the lion broke into a run. The canyon wall was close. With a graceful bound, the great cat sailed up onto a rocky ledge fifteen feet above the canyon floor. For an instant, the lion paused there, looking above him. Another leap upward would carry him to safety and escape. But above this rock ledge was a solid wall of smooth stone. There was no foothold where even an agile lion paw could find a purchase. The big lion of the Book Cliffs had made his last jump.

He turned and faced the hounds as they danced and barked below him. His cat lips wrinkled back in a snarl of defiance. He snarled, too, at the human hunters as we came close.

We could not help but stand there dumbly and admire the enormous cat form on the ledge above us. Roy did not have to say, "That's the biggest damn lion I've ever seen." Both men knew it was a record. The heavy shoulders and massive form of the cougar told of his enormous weight and size.

But the creeping cold of the Utah night was upon us. There was little time for admiration and no light for picture. Cass raised his short rifle. The sights were blurred in the near darkness as he centered on the white throat above him. The cougar growled again and struck downward at a dog that leaped up the rock face toward him. His green eyes seemed to glow in the darkness. He looked straight at Tony Medina; Tony was chanting in a low voice.

The last twilight of a winter sun seemed to outline the great lion. He stood snarling and looked off into the distance of time. A glow of unearthly light marked out the lion form from the dark rock behind. Roy Snyder, too, had his gun raised. Tony Medina held up his hand. Cass passed the Winchester to me. I shook my head. I held the gun at a downward angle. Roy, too, lowered his rifle. We were frozen with indecision. Perhaps it was Medina's chanting. Time stood still in the shadowed cliffs. Slowly the Medicine Lion turned and walked along the ledge. He looked up. With an effortless bound, he jumped up to a protruding rock we had not noticed. Bouncing from this, he doubled backward and up to another ledge no wider than a man's hand. The dogs fell silent. The lion looked down at us. His ears were forward and erect. With a slap of his furry tail, he was over the edge of the cliff and gone.

For once, Roy Snyder said nothing. Cass shook his head. Tony Medina still held his hand up with the palm upturned toward where the lion had disappeared.

Morning was graying the eastern sky when we at last found a way up the side of the canyon and retraced our steps to where we had left the horses. It was a dejected and frozen group that rode into camp and stiffly swung out of our cold saddles. During the night, Cass froze the toes of both his feet, and Roy and I were little better off.

Only Tony seemed pleased. Maybe his moccasins were warmer than any boots. "I say we no kill the Medicine Lion," Tony said as he started the fire with stiffened fingers. "Big Medicine stronger than bullets any time."

BIG BUCKS SLEEP LIGHTLY

CHAPTER VI

T ony Medina reined in his team of decrepit horses opposite our little camp. Tony's face was expressionless, as usual, and was rendered more so by a wide band of red paint that lay across his wrinkled cheeks and the bridge of his nose. His hat was round-crowned and wide-brimmed. Down his back dangled twin queues of hair braided with a white ribbon that marked Tony Medina as a conservative. Tony's clothes were shabby and shapeless, a fortuitous combination of store-bought Levi's and greasy buckskin. He wore hunting boots.

All these features we had noted on previous occasions, for we had hunted before with Tony Medina. The man who sat so patiently on the wagon box above us was the best hunter of Zia Pueblo. The Zia Indians spawned great hunters before white men ever brought powder and shot into these mountains of New Mexico.

As if to inquire why we had stopped him, Tony shifted the rifle that lay across his knees and looked down at us. The gun was a lever-action, octagonal-barreled relic, with a stock weathered white by fifty years of hunts such as this one. Indeed, everything about Tony Medina, from his listing wagon to the patched reins in his gnarled hands, looked antique, but time-tried and capable.

"Get down, Tony," Bill Burk said in his most affable tone. "We want to ask you where you get those big bucks every year." Bill Burk and I very much wanted to know where and how this mysterious Indian killed the monstrous mule deer that he always brought back to the pueblo. We had more than a passing curiosity as to why Tony Medina always brought back a huge deer. It was for this reason we had come into San Pablo Canyon in the heart of the Jemez Mountains of New Mexico.

For the last several seasons, my friend Burk and I had brought back buck deer that may be summed up in the words of our more tactful friends: "He isn't very big, but he'll make a fine piece of meat." Frankly, we were tired of "fine pieces of meat" with puny racks of antlers. This season, we were committed to hunt for one of the monsters that haunt the Jemez country, or come home empty-handed.

As if in answer to our preseason dream, we saw a branching beam of antler sticking out of the tailgate of Tony's disintegrating wagon. The dark spread of horn showed six tines above the splintered edge of the wagon, with promise of more below. Burk walked toward the vehicle with a quick step. We both fondled the spreading antlers of the colossal buck that lay at full length in the wagon bed. The gray body of the beast had rounded contours like a fat pony, and the neck and brisket were jet black and broad as a yearling steer. Tony Medina had done it again. On the second day of the season, he was jolting back over the old mining road with a monarch of a mule deer.

"Where do you Indians get these big bucks?" I asked with a sorry attempt at levity. I had known Tony Medina for years and had hunted with him on several mountain lion and bear hunts in the past. There is, however, always a certain strained relationship between those who have gotten game and those who have not done so. This relationship may be fawning. It is always envious.

"How do you get close to the big ones?" Bill Burk was saying as he rubbed his hand along one branching antler that stuck out toward him from the wagon. Questioning Indians is a technique all its own. As was to be expected, Tony shrugged his shoulders and looked solemn with his devil's mask of red paint over his face. For a full minute, he sat silent as though debating whether to answer us at all. One of the aged horses shifted his hooves on the rough stones of the road and the wagon creaked with the movement.

"Me shoot chief deer asleep," Tony said in his characteristic slow manner. At first I interpreted his cryptic words to mean that Indian huntsmen, with their painted faces, put the deer to sleep with the bullets from their ancient guns, which they certainly did, but Tony added a moment later, "Beeg bucks don't sleep so good." He pressed his fingers, still holding the reins, to the front of his wrinkled lips in a gesture that seemed to admonish us to silence even there while we talked in front of our camp. Bill and I looked at each other with quizzically raised eyebrows as the Indian wagon once again rumbled into motion and moved down the old road.

The last thing we could see of it and its occupants was the straight back of Tony Medina as he held himself stiffly against the lurching of the vehicle and the wide-spreading antlers of the magnificent deer that extended above the tailgate. "Hell," Burk exclaimed with a burst of bad temper, "I want a buck with a big rack of antlers like that Indian had in his wagon. That Tony Medina knows some secret place where there are only monster bucks."

"You've got to kill them asleep—and they don't sleep so good," I mimicked, trying to imitate the flat nasal tones of my Zia friend. Bill threw a piece of stovewood in my direction, and I retreated in confusion, tripping and falling flat over the tent rope as I backed up.

As Bill and I started up the first, long, slanting ridge on the side of San Pablo the next morning, we still talked about the matter in whispered accents. "How in hell can we find a big buck asleep if we can't even find one awake?" Bill remarked for the dozenth time. I glanced at him sideways with a look that one reserves for petulant children.

The sun had not yet topped the ridge above Miners' Mountain, and the cold air in the canyon was crisp around our ears and noses. Our labored breathing as we climbed the ridge was apparent in puffs of white in front of our mouths; the frost crystals crackled underfoot. There is nothing quite so still as a mountain canyon just before sunrise. Not an oak leaf shivered in the deathly still air. Far up on the slopes, a jay began to chatter as he anticipated the sun.

Suddenly, off to the left, there was the sound of hooves on hard ground. It was the measured thump, thump, thump of a deer bounding away on springing feet. No other animal in the woods makes a noise like that. I caught a glimpse of the gray body as it diagonaled between the boles of ghostly aspens off to one side.

Even in the dim light, it was apparent that the deer, as so many others that we had seen, carried no horns on its head. We dropped our tensed rifles and began to climb again. After a few moments, Burk paused and indicated he would like to hunt in the direction the doe had gone. "It looks good over there. It's open, with lots of buckbrush." He swung away parallel with the slope. It certainly would seem the best section to hunt in this part of the San Pablo, but some whim of tenacity kept me moving straight up the slope.

The crest of the highest ridge was still far above me where the Douglas firs were just dipping their tips in the red light of the earliest sunrise. The slope was steep and heavily timbered. Here on the north side, the snow lay inches deep and had not melted in the weak sunlight of November. Beneath the thickly growing trees, the forest floor was still and lifeless. No browse grew here. Certainly, it was not a place to find deer. I had some vague thought of topping out on the very summit of the topmost ridge, if only to see the other side.

On this steep northern slope the footing was treacherous. Dead underbranches of the trees snapped before my arms and body with pistolshot reports. Even beneath the snow blanket on the ground, dead twigs crunched and broke as I mounted the slope. The ground was frozen solid here, and I slid back as often as I advanced. It was a hopeless and entirely inane procedure.

But perhaps there is a part of God's attention riveted upon the hunter. Certain it is that there is a destiny that guides his steps. It was not sensible for me to mount the difficult side of San Pablo Canyon, but I did. About halfway up, I found a set of deer tracks in the snow. They were fresh. Each hard-dented print had disturbed the frost crystals on the snow's surface in much the same pattern as the mark of my hand beside it. It was obviously the track of a big buck and he was alone.

A single line of cuneiform prints in the snow led off before me, slanting upward beneath the trees. The prints were large enough to conjure up before me pictures of antlered heads that I had seen on taxidermists' walls. It must have been a mighty body that walked beneath these same fir trees, and that mighty body must have supported a heavy neck with antler beams as large around as a big man's wrist. A shiver of anticipation passed over me as I knelt on the slope and looked at the tracks. It was the same thrill that every hunter feels at the nearness of game. What would my Zia friend, Tony Medina, do in this situation?

I hitched along in the snow a few yards to look at the tracks. The big deer had been walking, picking his way carefully and placing his feet so as not to slip on the steep ground. "He's been feeding, and he came up this slope to bed down," I whispered to myself. I had become accustomed to whispering in the woods, even when voicing my own thought out loud. "To bed down." The phrase seemed remotely familiar, as though it meant something important. "I might find that deer asleep somewhere!" That was what the Zia Indian had said: "Kill them asleep."

With rising excitement, I slipped off my heavy coat and hung it on a convenient limb. I took several shells out of my pocket because they jangled together when I walked. I left even my hat, which had brushed so uncompromisingly against the twigs. These were the same preparations we habitually made when we were stalking something, whether it was a flock of alert Canadian geese along the Rio Grande or a herd of antelope in the open country. I even felt the need of a band of paint across my nose. The Zias had told me that the red color makes a hunter move noiselessly.

I started off along the track with as much caution as though the quarry were behind the next tree. The stillness was so intense in the crisp of the morning that no matter how slight a sound I made, it would ruin the show. I had a momentary vision of Tony Medina on the occasions when I had hunted with him. There was a slight hitch to his shoulders when he avoided a leaning tree trunk. He had a habit of lifting little branches in front of him and carefully placing them behind so that they made no noise whatsoever. Any Zia hunter would make a circuit of hundreds of yards to avoid a single down tree that might crackle underfoot.

I clawed my way up the San Pablo slope hoping I could emulate to some degree the example of these Indians. In a measure, I was glad I was alone. Two people make more noise than one. Also, there was no witness to the ludicrous attitudes that I assumed to remain silent. Twice I fell on my face with my gun buried in the snow before me. To break the fall, I would have had to grasp at dead branches, and that was unthinkable. In places I crawled, because the steep angle of the frozen ground gave little purchase to the edge of my shoe soles.

It was an exciting experience. Each additional vista of deer tracks before me seemed to give almost the satisfaction of viewing the game itself. No wonder Indians like hunting so well. They didn't blunder through the woods in places where deer might be. They followed tracks to places where deer were.

In this furtive manner, I arrived at the top of the ridge. During the stalk, the sun had climbed in the clear, blue sky to almost the position of noon. Sweat trickled down the small of my back as I stooped and wriggled beneath dead branches of the last trees on the slope. Drops of water from melting snow glistened on the barrel of the rifle. Again, I checked the muzzle for a snow plug. Certainly, this mighty mule deer would be lying just at the peak of the slope, looking back down his trail. Into the full sunlight of the crest I crawled on hands and knees, expecting any moment to see my quarry face to face.

Here the trees were wider spaced, and a parklike vista of stately yellow pines spread before me. The snow had melted away here, leaving the needle-covered ground bare except for fluffy, white patches in the shade near the trunks. The big buck tracks led through the scattered patches of snow and then onto pine needles altogether. I crawled forward on my knees, feeling again a thrill of anticipation. I thrust my rifle out before me.

But the open pine woods were as silent as the snowy slope below had been. I could see every inch of forest floor and there was nothing. There was also, on the springy pine needles, no indication of the direction in which the great buck had gone.

I straightened up. I even essayed a few careless steps beneath the pine trees, abandoning the difficult silence that had bound me so long. Perhaps I might circle the top of the ridge and by chance bump into something. There was no reason to continue my careful stalk. It was now again the same old system that Bill had called the "stagger and search method."

On the other side of the San Pablo ridge, several minor ridges led away like the fingers of a giant hand. The crests of these spurs were quite visible through the open trees. All of these places were bare of snow, however, and I put my rifle over my shoulder and started off with a rapid step. By circling the crests of these ridges, I proposed to cover all of this high country quickly and then descend again to more profitable territory. My great stalk had been a complete bust, but the sun was warm on my back as I walked. A canyon wren trilled some place below me, and a buzzard circled against the perfect blue of the sky. These are the things that we hunt, after all.

Between two of the spur ridges on the far side was a thick clump of young pines and dwarf oaks all growing together. In the shade of this verdure, little tablecloth patches of snow lingered, secure from the sun. As I stepped on each of these, the granular stuff that had thawed and frozen again crunched a little, and I glanced down involuntarily to see where I might step to make no sound. There, on the edge of one of these patches, was a lump of snow detached from the rest. It was a fresh fragment, not at all melted, and yet it had not come from my own careless foot. I crouched low and looked ahead. There it was again, in the shade of a small pine tree ahead of me, the perfect print of a monster buck deer. It was the same that I had followed all that fruitless morning.

So this was the way he had come. I brought the rifle up over my elbow, tensed again. But, as before, these open woods seemed as still as death. Certainly there was no other living thing on that isolated ridge except myself. Not a breath of wind moved the pine limbs or brown oak leaves before me. Out of the corner of my eye, I saw something shake in the thicket. It was not a branch of the stunted trees, for they were as still as before. The movement was as disturbing as the unremembered name of a dear friend. There it was again, the barest flick of motion through the screen of the tree clump.

Still crouching on the edge of the snow, I laid the rifle across my knees, holding it close to my body, and worked my field glass out of the front of my shirt where I had tucked it to prevent its swinging. I focused the lenses up close to include the thickest mass of brush, only thirty or forty yards away. As the focus sprang into clarity, I saw a shape that was not like the bole of a pine tree or any vegetable thing. It was a shape pointed at the end and thick in the middle like a large seed pod. There it was again! It flicked forward and back. It was an ear. That was it! The ear of a mule deer.

And there was the head lying at full length on the ground. Gradually I picked out, with great difficulty, parts of the deer's body. It was a magnificent shape, rounded and with the proportions of a gray Missouri mule. "This must be the one," ran through my mind again and again, "and he's asleep. He's not even looking my way," for the gray nose of the beast was turned in the opposite direction. It was only the ear that moved, occasionally, with some spasmodic twitching, to betray the deer's presence. But, strain as I might, I could see no indication of any antler whatsoever.

My excitement turned to near panic. Here was a gigantic mule deer not forty yards from me and I could make out no horns! If it was a doe, she was a colossus of her kind. I shifted my weight ever so little to move my head to the side, striving for some new vista through the thick branches. The crusted snow squeaked beneath my boot, and I winced as though someone had struck me. I peered again through the brush and the gray ear moved back and forth more vigorously than before. Slowly I laid the rifle on the pine needles beside the snow patch and shifted on hands and knees to one side. The movement took an eternity. There was no other solution. I shifted perhaps three yards to the right. From here, a small opening promised a better view.

Again I put the glass to my eyes and swept it forward to cover the form of the sleeping deer. In the circle of the lenses this time were only oak leaves, dry and sear, and long clumps of pine needles hanging gracefully from the young trees. I could not locate the gray outline of the ear or make out any part of the body, yet the huge deer must be there. I thought I could make out some slim trunks of young trees in the midst of the clump, which I had not noticed in my previous inspection. With a sudden impulse, I moved the glass upward to increase the field.

There he was! Standing on all four feet and looking straight at me! How the deer had gotten up so silently, I will never know. The animal hadn't rustled a twig or moved a leaf. The slim stems that I had followed with my glass were his legs, and I could see the gray body with the arching neck quite plainly without the aid of my lenses.

In one trembling movement, I swept the glass to the deer's head, dimly outlined behind the interlacing pine needles and leaves. The branches of one small pine crossed agonizingly just above the deer's ears and the top of his head was as blank as before. I could not make out a vestige of a horn. It simply could not be a doe. No doe would act that way. No doe could have that bulk, could be that black on neck and brisket. The deer was as thick through the body as a horse, and as sexless as a T-bone steak.

I looked at the head again. As I did so, the deer moved, ever so slightly, perhaps to see me better through the foliage. Then I saw them! With the magnification blurring the many intervening sticks, I saw two black pillars on top of the animal's head, and then, with the sudden clarity of a vision, the horns appeared above a low place in the brush. The points of many-branching tines arched a yard apart over the buck's head.

The deer was a monster, and I had wasted precious moments goggling at him like any novice with a vicious case of buck fever. The glass dropped unheeded and I ran my hand slowly over my thigh groping for the rifle in the pine needles. My fingers touched the cold steel and pulled off the safety as I raised the weapon jerkily with excitement. The sights came into line. Where the heart would be was a small, thick bush, heavy enough to make the shot uncertain. The neck would be better.

But there comes a time when fortune's patience runs out. I had dallied too long with the golden opportunity of my Indian stalk. The deer gave me a whistling snort as only a great buck can when he sees danger close. The fanning ears dropped back and the magnificent head jerked with the first movement of the bound. Even as the great body trembled and slid before my sights, I desperately pulled the trigger. The noise of the shot was like a blast in that quiet wood. It was a blast that seemed to destroy the vision that had been before me. With the noise of the shot and the recoil of the gun against my shoulder, the great buck simply disappeared. He did not fall. I saw no movement in the brush that might be an animal kicking his last against the oak stems. My ears rang with the reverberation of the shot, but there was no sound of running hooves. The magnificent mule deer had simply disappeared.

For a fleeting moment I thought that perhaps some insanity had overcome me, some illusory sickness that afflicts hunters who have followed deer tracks too long. In that lonely place, some treacherous pine snag may have looked and acted like a monstrous mule deer. I had heard that there were mirages on snow even in the mountains.

Still with these numbing thoughts troubling me, I walked forward into the thicket where I thought I had seen a big buck asleep. I reached the spot where the deer had lain. Sure enough, there was a bed. That much was real, at least, but there was no drop of blood, no single indication that the big buck had been hurt or that I had fired a shot at him at point-blank range. I circled the pine needles around the thicket in the hollow. Just one drop of blood showed that it was not a dream. Just one scuffed print where sharp hooves had turned up the frozen mold would indicate at least that the deer had bounded away. There was not a single mark. The great animal was a figment of the imagination, a wraith of the Jemez forest. He had simply vanished.

I remember well that the next thought that occurred to me was that I would make no mention of this affair to Bill Burk. Certainly, he would have no mercy upon me if I described this fairy deer, a ghost buck that made tracks on the snow but disappeared into solid pine trees.

I turned for a last look at the little swale. The scenery looked real enough. The young pines and the oak scrub and the little patches of snow were commonplace and familiar. Beyond the thicket where I had fired the shot, a rotted oak limb protruded from the pine needles. Wait! That snag was smooth and it branched at the top into six tapering points.

As I ran forward, I saw the other antler and the gray of the head and the muzzle, just over the slope. The huge dark body lay still, and the feet were bunched together as though the buck had stretched out on the warm pine needles and fallen asleep. But as I came close, I saw a dark stain in the hair behind his shoulder. The gray-green eyes of the noble animal were already opaque with the cloudiness of death.

"Tony Medina has a good system," I told Bill Burk that evening as we sat before the fire. "He's entirely right about the bucks being light sleepers. As a matter of fact, I think a broad band of red paint across the face is the only sure way."

BIG BASE BLACKIE

CHAPTER VII

B ig Base Blackie was a monarch of the mountains. I do not recall how we came to call him by that name, or exactly when, for we had caught only one short glimpse of the bear in the three years that we had tracked and harried him through the rough Jemez canyons of New Mexico. It is true that his posterior was of remarkable size, but the really huge parts of his anatomy were his feet, and we were looking at the impression of one of them at that very moment.

"Look at the print of that paw!" Cass Goodner ejaculated excitedly, as he tested the imprint with his outstretched fingers. "It's as big as the number four shoe on a plow-horse, and just as deep."

"Big Base got big foot, too," Tony Chenana said quietly as he also leaned over the impression. Tony was an Indian from the neighboring village of Jemez. The Pueblo Indians are all hunters and have taken game out of these same mountains for the last thousand years. To the Jemez Indians, however, bears are different from other animals. The black bruins of the Jemez Mountains contain such powerful spirit medicine that they may not be hunted by ordinary men or killed in an ordinary manner. But Tony Chenana was no ordinary Indian. It is true that he was short and stocky in build, as are most of the Jemez people. He seemed light of muscle and placid of face, as though he had neither the fortitude nor the determination to enter upon so hazardous a process as the pursuit of a great black bear.

The look of quietude on Tony's wrinkled features, however, was deceiving to a degree. The dark eyes in his folded cheeks took in every detail of the wild mountain scene around us and read every bit of the information that could be derived from the print of the black bear in the soft forest mold at our feet. Tony Chenana was the finest tracker in the whole pueblo of trackers. He could follow a deer or a bear for a week, without the aid of dogs, and tell you at the end everything the animal had done.

Tony knelt closer, although he did not place his hand in the bear prints as Cass Goodner had done before him. The vibrating power that the forest bears radiate from their bodies may come from their tracks as well. No Jemez Indian will step in the tracks of a bear or even touch the imprint with his hand.

"It's Big Base," Tony declared with his usual conservation of word matter. He nodded his head vigorously up and down to add emphasis to his declaration, and the bright cerise band of ribbon that he had tied around his hair gleamed like a firefly in the gathering darkness.

We turned slowly and walked back to our camp at the mouth of San Miguel Canyon, meanwhile discussing the big bear and how we might catch him this year.

We had first run him three years ago in these same canyons. San Pablo and San Miguel are both remarkable scars on the south side of the Jemez Mountains. Both of these clefts are rocky and rough as only Western canyons can be, where nature has faulted and thrust the tortured rocks into a jumble of cliffs, dikes, and knife edges through which the tumbling waters of the mountain streams have worn a devious and zigzag descent.

Throughout this maze of colored ledges and red-rock pinnacles, there grow clumps of Gambel oak, whose twining roots suck the moisture from the pockets of rich volcanic soil that rest between the stones. On the stiff branches of these same oaks grow the succulent acorns in the fall of the year that bring the black bears of the Jemez to this rock garden of the gods. It is both a refuge and a feeding place for them, but for men and dogs it is a rocky, cliff-dissected nightmare that makes all hunting difficult and fast movement impossible. When these feeding bruins are startled into flight by keen-nosed dogs and determined men behind them, the bears will run for a while over this rough terrain and, at last, will climb a tree and sit there panting on a big limb while they catch their bear breath, and the men with their rifles draw close.

All this is normal and the way black bears should react in the fall when they have eaten the ripe acorns and made ready for their hibernation. But Big Base Blackie, our special friend of these same colorful canyons, had not heard of this orthodoxy. As far as we were aware, this one black bear had never climbed a tree in his life, and when we first made his acquaintance, he had obviously no intention of beginning.

In two seasons of heart-breaking effort in these rough canyons, we followed this bear half a dozen times, and his tactics were always the same. He always ran in a straight line and at full speed and never stopped. We caught a glimpse of the round contours of his mountainous back on only one occasion, and we saw that his hide was jet black. Our hounds indubitably saw him many times, but it did them no good, nor ourselves either, for that matter. On every occasion, the bear led us deep into the heart of the Jemez canyon country and invariably left us there, exhausted and disgruntled. Usually, we had the job of carrying out our saddles on our own backs and sometimes a footsore hound or two as well.

At this juncture in our troubled hunting affairs, we enlisted the aid of Tony Chenana, who is known among a tribe of hunters as the greatest hunter of them all. Cass and I had an idea that with the skill of this mountain-bred Indian we might match the wiles of a certain black bear that had derived his stratagems from these same cliffs and canyons. We put Tony into camp in San Miguel Canyon with simple instructions to keep track of Big Base Blackie and find out his daily movements, if he could. Tony Chenana was to spy on the bear. Cass and I immediately felt that with this intelligence our next attempt into these rough canyons would be a different story.

On a certain Friday afternoon, our pickup labored up the old mining road that led into the mouth of San Miguel Canyon. Within the mouth of the canyon is a small flat of a few acres where some dozens of years ago hopeful men with a gleam of gold in their eyes had built a smelter of stone and fitted it with furnaces and chimneys. These man-made scars of the mining era had long ago begun to heal. The minerals of San Miguel had been transitory, and the smelter soon fell into disuse and then into decay. Cottonwood trees now grew around the fallen stone masonry.

Tony's small lean-to was built beneath one of these same colorful trees. Tony himself was in a sour mood. "You leave me no gun to shoot turkeys. All around, many turkeys, everywhere turkeys." Tony spread his hands expansively to indicate the numbers of wild turkeys that might be in these canyons. Even as he spoke, we heard the perk, perk, perk of a group of hens as they came down to water at the spring by the old smelter. Tony pointed them out to us with his air of "see there what you have done to me." He had stuck an eagle feather in the band of cloth around his head for this special occasion, and he nodded this emphatically.

"Damn the turkeys!" Cass said irritably. "What about the bear?"

"Oh, him," Tony answered laconically and straightened the eagle feather on his head with pensive fingers.

Late that night, we managed to wrest some information from our taciturn friend concerning the habits of the bear. "Him feed all day, every day on ridge—there!" Tony pointed behind him into the darkness beyond our campfire. "He not eat in night. Rest belly. Every morning can run far."

So that was it! Instead of feeding by night and resting by day, Big Base Blackie raked his cavernous jaws full of acorns during the daylight hours and slept at night, just as we humans do.

Cass and I talked almost all night. In turn, we concocted and rejected a dozen plans of attack. None of them seemed to have a chance of success. We knew where the bear was, but we also knew, just as clearly, that he would run away from us as before. We might possibly get in front of him somewhere, but this seemed an outside chance in that thick country, and we might be years getting a shot at the monster bear by hit-or-miss methods.

Sometime late in the night, we ceased our talk and lay quiet. A wind began to come up, and the branches of the cottonwoods swayed above us and jerked the vines of the woodbine this way and that with a rustling sound. The wind from the west would bring a storm. It always did. If we had a storm, there would be no hunt at all. We wouldn't even have a chance, I thought as I fell asleep.

Hunting hopes rise highest in the dawn light, just as the coffeepot comes to a boil. The wind still blew and stirred the ashes from the fire, but the real storm had not yet broken. It might be another day or two.

"I've got an idea," Cass said suddenly, as he warmed the metal bit of his bridle at the fire. "It doesn't do us any good to trail that bear. He'll hear the hounds and be a mile away before we even get started." Cass threw his nose into the wind, as though he himself were a hound taking the scent of the wild things that might be down-canyon in the breeze. "Let's go right to him," he said mystically.

Tony Chenana seemed to understand these inexplicable statements, for he started up the trail as though he knew exactly what to do. But finding a big bear with such exactitude in the middle of a few hundred square miles of mountain country seemed quite a trick to me.

As we rode, Cass leaned occasionally from the saddle to question Tony, who trotted along ahead of the horses. I crowded up on these occasions to find out, if I could, what our master stratagem would be. Tony Chenana told exactly where he had followed Big Base Blackie on a single ridge of thick-growing oak that lay near the head of San Miguel Canyon. We could see the ridge now, as the light grew stronger over the mountain, and Tony pointed out where the bear fed on the western slope of the place where the oak grew thickest.

As we looked in the distance, the wind was tossing the trees in ripples over the surface of the slope like a breeze over acres of ripe grain. But those stalks on that mountainside were not wheat straws; they were gnarled oak limbs as thick as a man's leg and as high in places as the head of a mounted horseman. Winter snows in these wild places had, in many years past, matted much of the oak down so that it grew at angles from the ground that nurtured it. I had been in masses of Gambel oak before, and it was a sorry experience. A man on horseback cannot force his way through those unresisting limbs, and even on foot, it is an ordeal.

Cass sat his horse for a moment and looked at the situation. I thought at first he might be hoping for a glimpse of the big black bear in those acres of tossing oaks, but a thousand bears could have successfully hidden in the windswept maze. No, Cass was again testing the wind, as though to make certain of its direction. This done, he touched his horse with his spurs and whistled up the dogs around the legs of the horses. He twitched his bridle reins to the right, and we headed in a wide sweep as though to circle the oak slope where the bear lived.

"Cass," I called a couple of times over the noise of the thrashing branches around us, "don't you think we ought to bore in and get the dogs in those oaks?" I'm afraid most of my questions were whipped away in the wind, but Cass only waved his gloved hand over his shoulder and beckoned me on. I soon saw that we were mounting the crest of the spur ridge well to the east of the place that Tony had pointed out to us. Here the oaks were thinner, and there were occasional pine trees, around which we threaded our horses. Through the small glades we trotted our mounts, stopping here and there to negotiate some difficult rock pile or lava ledge that was hidden by the oak. I saw little use in climbing where we were, for we were too far to one side, by several yards, of the spot where the bear stayed.

Again Cass tested the wind that blew up the face of the slope toward us, tossing the rustling oak leaves on our faces as we rode. I, too, turned my face into the wind. That was it! I looked directly down the oak slope where Tony Chenana had, for the past five days, tracked the big bear and marked its sleeping places. We wouldn't have to trail Big Base Blackie. Our dogs would wind him.

As if in answer to my thought, Sissy, our red-colored lead dog, threw up her head and turned her nose into the wind. Cass jerked his horse to a stop so that his mount would not step on the dog. At the same time, he pulled one foot out of the stirrup as though ready to dismount on the instant. Rusty and Jumbo, too, had their noses in the air and wrinkled their black nostrils this way and that, as though feeling for some invisible substance that rode the wind currents that filtered through the twisted oak stems on the slope of the mountain. Then Sissy gave tongue in one ecstatic yelp, and she was off.

In a flash, Cass was out of the saddle unnecking the younger dogs as the whole hound pack streamed down through the oaks in a wild, barking melee. I took time only to wrench my rifle from the boot under the stirrup fender, and I was off after them. There was no use in trying to ride a horse through that oaken jungle. I caught a glimpse or two of the dogs ahead. No hound had a nose to the ground, but all ran with heads in the air and yelped and howled ecstatically, according to their kind. In another moment, there were only hound voices down there in the oak trees and Cass and I were fighting and clawing to make our way through the thickets.

Jemez oak would be the ideal situation for a fiendish football coach to train his squad. Anyone who races through those thickets must bend, twist, crawl, and leap all in one movement. The raking twigs of the awful stuff are as unresisting as iron wire and as clawing as steel hooks.

After a few moments of clawing progress, we stopped for a few seconds to listen. Tony Chenana had disappeared somewhere. Cass and I were alone in a world of twisted black oak trunks sticking out at every crazy angle around us and thrashing russet-colored leaves above our heads. But, through the ceaseless noise of the wind in the dry foliage, there was the roar of the dogs somewhere down the slope. Their barking had blended into one roar of sound, mixed here and there with yelps and growls, and one and then another dog darted in to snap at the bear. They were fighting and running.

Cass and I, together, started again through the oak branches and trunks at a scrambling run. We tripped and fell often but were up and away again with never a grunt of pain. I had fallen for perhaps the dozenth time and twisted as I fell to protect the rifle that I carried. My hat was gone, torn off back there somewhere when I ducked beneath a low-slanting tree. Half of my hunting coat was ripped away, and one canvas pocket hung downward at my side like a lifeless hound's ear, but I bore on, fending the branches from my face and clawing through the growth.

There was no need to stop and listen for the dogs now. They were close, very close, in the welter of oak branches ahead. Still the hounds growled and surged, and I could hear, mixed with the dog voices, the wheezing of a larger animal and the bubbling growls that came from his throat.

There they were, just a few yards away. I saw first a dog's hind leg; then it disappeared. There was another flash of movement, which might have been anything as it passed across a small opening between the trees. I moved forward, but the close-growing trunks and moving limbs were dense before me.

Suddenly, a whole oak in the midst of the moving maelstrom of sound broke in the middle and toppled away like a straw of wheat before the blade of a sickle. A mighty black paw had hit the thing in the middle and broken it clear off, as though the tough oak had, indeed, been a straw. There was a glimpse of the bear's head, round, with his ears laid back and the size of a bushel basket. Then it was gone again, as the animal lunged toward the dogs and made great sweeping motions before him with his mighty paws. I thrust the rifle forward, but there were still oaks and dancing dogs in the way.

There was no chance, in that sea of oak, to shoot at the bear unless I actually stood in the middle of the fight. I came within yards of the antagonists, battling there in the oak, and another tree went down as the panting bodies hurtled against it from below.

Then, through the noise and the sound of splintering wood, the bear saw or smelled me. I do not know which. He paused, half-raised on his hind legs, and looked over the backs of the dancing hounds directly into my eyes. Big Base Blackie had dark, intelligent eyes with little red rims, as though he had not slept well the night before. For a single instant, his ears went forward, as if to telegraph to his bear brain that a hated man-thing stood there in the oak, so menacing and close. Then he was gone.

He had pivoted on his mighty feet, as nimble as a dancing master, and was off down through the oaks before I could get my rifle to my shoulder. I thumbed back the hammer quickly and swung the barrel ahead to try to cover some slight gap between the oak trees down the slope where a patch of black fur might show for an instant. There it was! Crack! The steel-shod butt of the little carbine jerked back against my shoulder. I had fired like a shotgunner hoping to lead a ruffed grouse that flushed in thick timber. I thought I saw a puff of black hair fly, but I wasn't sure. Then the fight was gone. The bear, the dogs—all were swallowed again by the thrashing oaks.

I reloaded slowly, thinking that I had missed a lifetime chance at one of the largest bears I had ever seen. Just then, Cass stuck his head out from among the oaks and looked at me questioningly. I shook my head in the negative, and we turned down the hill together.

We could easily follow the path of the adversaries as they passed down the slope by the skinned trunks and splintered branches in the wake of the antagonists. Then I saw a drop of blood. Of course, it might be from the foot of some luckless hound that had been hurt in the struggle, but it looked dark and red, as though it came from a deeper wound. We quickened our steps, even as the sound of the dogs below roared out anew between gusts of the fitful wind blowing over the slope.

"They've got him stopped," Cass yelled in my ear, and, at the same time, he jerked me roughly on. There were, at the very bottom of that awful, oaken slope, a few scattered pines and spruces that stood as the advance guard of the forest in the canyon bottom, which was fighting unsuccessfully with the oaks of the upper slopes. It was from these scattered trees that the noise came, the sound of frantic hounds and the snapping jaws of a beleaguered bear. Big Base Blackie should have been across the canyon by this time. Something must be wrong.

Even as we ran through the last of the oaks at the foot of the slope, we saw a black bulk emerge over the tops of the brush at the base of one of the trees. A massive paw reached up and clutched the bark at one side of the bole of a pine that grew by itself. Then another mighty paw reached out on the other side, and the head of the bear appeared as he hitched himself up the trunk of the tree.

As a telephone lineman climbs a pole, Big Base Blackie slowly and deliberately pulled himself up the trunk of the pine as we drew close. There seemed something fateful and ominous about his movements. Even though a frantic hound chewed and wrestled at his hindquarters as he ascended, he did not hurry.

Another dog, wild with excitement, climbed up a small oak that grew near the base of the larger pine. Forgetting, in the heat of the moment, that hound paws are not adapted to climbing, this particular dog started to scale the tree and launched himself onto the black form of the bear above. For a moment, the hound's teeth closed on the ham of the animal's trunk and a handful of black hair came away in the dog's mouth as the audacious hound fell in a heap among his companions. But the great black bear, spread-eagled against the pine, seemed not to notice these petty irritations and, with tremendous heaves of rippling muscle beneath his black fur, pulled himself upward and onto a huge limb that grew about twenty feet above the ground.

Big Base Blackie had climbed his last tree, or possibly his only tree, so far as we knew. Every motion that he made seemed to indicate that he, also, was sure this was the end. We found out later that in his climb, Blackie had pulled out four of his claws completely with the effort of hoisting his huge bulk up the trunk of that lonely pine.

He draped his flabby bear body over the big pine limb in an awkward manner, as though he were unused to such heights and they ill-suited his dignity. For the first time, we could truly appreciate the mass of fat and bone and muscle that was this particular bear. Then, as we looked and admired, I saw the slow drip of dark blood as it ran down the fur of the bear's belly onto the pine limb and splashed in bright splotches on the oak leaves beneath the tree.

Only once, Big Base Blackie swept his massive head around and looked full at us as we stood on the slope. Again, he laid his ears back and bared his gleaming teeth in one last gesture of defiance. He opened wide those cavernous jaws that could have crushed any one of us in a single bite. Then he closed jaws and teeth together with a resounding slam, like the noise of a closing steel door. That was all.

The blank eyes seemed to film over with the cloudiness that comes as every being sees beyond the curtain that separates this world from the next. The proud head of Big Base Blackie sank low on the limb as I fired a merciful shot through the bulky neck. The great body tumbled out of the tree and hit the ground with a thump that seemed to shake the earth and very nearly killed one of the dogs.

News of the death of the big bear seemed to have reached the little native village of San Ysidro even before we ourselves got there. There is a mysterious intelligence that travels with the speed of radio over these wilderness distances. A friendly native from this place offered to help us load the bear and get him out of San Miguel Canyon back to our camp.

We took, for this purpose, a block and tackle and procured the offices of a heavy plow horse of the Percheron variety, whose broad back, we hoped, could stand the weight of this carcass. Four of us, each grasping a limp paw of the late Big Base Blackie, could not begin to stir the carcass from the ground. We tugged and dragged the dead animal to a place where we could bring the block and tackle into play and hoist him into the air.

As we worked and sweated over the carcass, we made frequent bets with one another that the body would weigh over 500 pounds. By the time we had loaded the massive animal onto the protesting horse and saw the Percheron stagger beneath the dead weight of the bear, our estimates of the gross tonnage of Big Base Blackie were above the 550 pound mark. But, as it turned out later, we had the "big eye," as Cass called it.

Hog-dressed, on the stock scales of Albuquerque the next day, Big Base Blackie tallied exactly 423 pounds. He was a full-grown male, in prime condition and with perfect teeth. But, so far as I'm concerned, it was not the statistics of Blackie that made him our greatest achievement. He was more than just a monster bear. He was, as Tony Chenana, said, "a strong medicine bear." I can feel the power of his spirit whenever I lay my hand on the long hair of his hide and think, again, of the end of a gallant animal.

FOUR AGAINST FOUR

CHAPTER VIII

The story is often told among the Rio Grande Pueblos of this great fight. All the storytellers refer to the incident as "Four against Four." The tale was first told me by Ramondo Sanchez, a San Felipe Indian and a nephew of Felipe Sanchez, who died so bravely beneath the paw of the female grizzly. It was Ramondo who showed me the ledge in Peralta Canyon where the great bear fight took place. There is a shrine there, and from time to time, prayer plumes are left upon it to commemorate the event.

If the hunters had been lesser men, there might have been no encounter and no carnage. But these four—Armando, the leader, Felipe Sanchez, Bent Willow, and Tony Eagle Tail—had reputations to uphold. A good reputation can be a stern master. Each of these hunters had piled at least twenty pairs of deer antlers on the roof of his house to show his prowess. Even Bent Willow, the youngest of the group, already had been initiated into the Hunt Society and was recognized in San Felipe Pueblo as a tracker of great ability.

It was not that the four Indians were following the grizzlies. They would not have done so under any circumstances. All the Pueblo Indians, including the San Felipes, have a wholesome respect for bears and especially for the silver-tipped grizzlies that occasionally stalked through their hunting grounds. Long ago, the San Felipe people had learned the potency of all bears. Any Pueblo child can tell you that these animals, more than all others, radiate powerful medicine from their bodies that can contaminate any human that touches them. No San Felipe will even step in a bear track if he can help it.

Armando, being a skillful hunter, never would have entered the same canyon with the grizzly if he had seen her sign. As it was, their search for deer had been unsuccessful and the four hunters were returning to the Pueblo along a trail that led down from the cliffs. There was no warning that a grizzly was even in the country. There was no sound or even a premonition.

The cliffs of the Jemez Mountains above San Felipe Pueblo are made of black lava that spewed in past geological ages from the volcanic crater of the Valle Grande, or Big Valley. These cliffs descend from the mountain in levels like gigantic stairs, each one representing an individual lava flow that puddled there in molten form and then hardened into stone. Straight-sided canyons have long ago cut through the caprock to break these lava flows into a series of isolated mesas and scallops. The sides of the canyon are marked here and there by ledges and offsets that represent the levels of these same rock flows, one on top of the other, that came from the parent volcano. And over the whole of this rough terrain, nature long ago spread a healing cover of pines and furs. Mountain mahogany grows in lush clumps. On the tops of the mesas made by lava, the deer feed on the buck brush and hide securely in the rough brakes. Along the ledges and in the canyons, too, there is game. A volcanic country is a rich country, and the San Felipes had one of the best and most rewarding hunting grounds of any of the Pueblos along the Rio Grande.

The trail the hunters followed led along a ledge that skirted the side of Peralta Canyon. Not only was it a shortcut to the Pueblo, but also the hunters still hoped they could yet bring down a deer with the use of this strategy.

Armando and Felipe were armed with guns. These were antiquated and ineffective Winchester models. At that particular time, before the turn of the twentieth century, these rifles were regarded as the latest development. Both Armando and Felipe carried their guns with a certain pride. Felipe had attached a yellow eagle feather to the neck of the stock of his weapon. In this way, the rifle would kill as the eagle does, swiftly and without warning. The other two, Bent Willow and Tony Eagle Tail, carried bows and quivers of arrows. The arrows were tipped with scraps of iron that the two hunters had salvaged from the rims of old wagonwheels. At short range, and in the hands of a powerful man, the arrows were almost as effective as slow-moving bullets.

By skirting the ledges of the canyon, the hunters hoped to find a deer feeding in the mahogany brush below them. The height gave them an advantage. Often, these skillful hunters had stalked deer while they were feeding and shot them before the animals were aware of the presence of humans.

Armando, with his three companions close behind him, trod silently and looked down. The wind of the early evening moved up along the rock wall, so that any deer feeding below in the canyon bottom could not scent the nearness of danger.

Perhaps it was a slight sound that warned the hunters—the rattle of dry leaves—or the shuffling of a padded foot against the rough rock. Whatever it was, Armando whirled and there was the grizzly before him. The great bear was on the same ledge and no further away than Armando could reach by extending the barrel of his rifle with one arm. The bear reared on her hind legs, and Armando saw the rows of dry teats on her belly and the crowding forms of three other bears behind her. They were big cubs, perhaps a year and a half old, but still with their mother.

Grizzlies do not stand on their hind legs to attack. This act showed that the she-bear was as startled as the Indians. If only the four San Felipes had been cowards and not the hunters they were, they might have turned and fled. Or if the grizzly had not been typical of her kind, she, too, might have saved the situation. Coincidence could not have brought together antagonists more poorly suited to flight.

Armando threw up the octagonal-barreled rifle, thumbed back the hammer, and fired point-blank at the grizzly's chest. The Winchester roared and jerked back along his arm. The muzzle was so close that he actually saw the dark-colored hair blanch and burn from the powder blast. The grizzly reeled back, then swayed toward Armando and fell forward upon him.

Felipe Sanchez and the others watched in horror as the shebear crushed Armando. Before the other Indians could fire a shot, the massive paws of the monster gathered Armando's head and carried it to her mouth like a child embracing a ball. The grizzly's jaw opened wide. There was a crunch of bone. Armando screamed. The shebear bit through his head with as little effort as if she were mouthing a robin's egg. The body fell away. Armando's feet moved a little without any kind of purpose or direction.

The she-grizzly stepped over the bloody form and raised her head. There was red on her teeth. The odds were three against four now.

Bent Willow had crowded forward to shoot an arrow, but the shaft never left his bow. Armando's dying scream had frozen his will. His every nerve urged flight. Tony Eagle Tail also seemed numbed by the nearness of death and did not move.

Felipe fired once, twice. The big grizzly fixed her reddened eyes upon him and lunged forward. Behind her came her offspring. The cubs were only slightly smaller than their mother, with dispositions just as deadly.

Bent Willow shrank back and looked behind him at the open ledge, the way they had come. Felipe Sanchez shouted the scalping cry. The she-grizzly roared. Bent Willow hesitated with his feet poised for flight. The pull of loyalty—the stain of cowardice. He could not leave his friends in a fight.

Felipe fired at the demon face that came straight at him. One of the red-rimmed eyes seemed to wink out. Felipe knew that if those hooked claws found his own flesh, he, too, would die between the awful teeth. There seemed to be two bears before him. Felipe fired wildly at the second of the two apparitions. Tony Eagle Tail sent an ineffective arrow into the melee from behind. The strings of indecision seemed to pull Bent Willow in two directions at the same time.

Again and again, Felipe Sanchez levered shells into the chamber of his gun and fired without aiming. One soft-lead bullet hit the foremost of the younger bears in the neck. A vertebra snapped. The cub went limp and rolled over into the brink of the ledge, striking against the treetops in the canyon below.

Felipe thrust the rifle forward at the she-bear. The hammer clicked on the empty chamber.

Frantically, he pawed at the bullet pouch that hung under his shoulder. He had his fingers on three or four brass cartridges when a dark paw swept from the side. There was a thud. The bright brass shells spurted from Felipe's hand as the blow fell. The sweeping paw seemed to break him in two, and he went down like a stalk of wheat before a scythe. He cried out only once as the blow broke through the middle of his body. Then he rolled, lifeless, and lay face down on the rock.

Bent Willow and Tony Eagle Tail had already fitted new arrows to their bowstrings, but they stood immobile.

As the combatants faced each other there on the narrow ledge, the odds were three grizzlies against two Indians. While the hunters struggled against the panic that pumped through their veins, the gods of chance tipped the balance. The she-grizzly vomited blood from her throat. One of the bullets had pierced her lungs. A red spot in the hair on her side widened slowly and bubbled as she breathed. One of her eyes was gone, but the other still blazed fury.

She lurched forward toward Eagle Tail, who was in front. He gave a little before her charge. Nothing could save him if the bear's wide-reaching paws gathered him in. Suddenly, she halted in midmotion.

One front paw crumpled beneath her, as though she had tripped on a wire. Then, slowly, she sank forward until her snout rested on the rock. She turned her blazing eye toward the two Indians, then that red-rimmed window of a hateful soul seemed to cloud over. The great carcass rolled on its side and was still.

Tony Eagle Tail squared his shoulders with decision. The great she-bear was dead. "Do you think we can get the rifle?" he asked of Bent Willow behind him. The Winchester lay just beyond Felipe's dead hand. Two or three shiny shells were also scattered there.

The two hunters saw the smaller bears hesitate when their mother died. The foremost cub seemed almost mild-mannered and by his actions indicated surprise and bewilderment rather than the usual ferocity of his kind.

The two remaining bears advanced forward a few steps. Tony Eagle Tail edged toward the fallen gun. The foremost grizzly was close beside the carcass of the fallen female. Tony crouched and calculated his distance from the Winchester. He would have not only to snatch the gun but to pick up a cartridge or two as well. Bent Willow faced the enemy and held his bow ready.

Suddenly, the bear stood up on his hind legs. It was not an act of attack, but the action startled Eagle Tail. Quickly he bent the bow, leveled the iron-shod arrow at the grizzly's chest, and released the string. His aim was good—too good, perhaps. The shaft hit the bear in the middle of his body where the keel of the breast forms a ridge of bone and cartilage. The arrow stuck there, not driving deeply, although the grizzly staggered back at the impact.

"Oof!" The sound came from between the curling lips of the bear. If the young grizzly had not been fighting mad before, the stinging arrow decided the issue. It was the rising anger of an animal whose ancestors had always been touchy.

Eagle Tail was already reaching for another shaft from the quiver behind his shoulder when the first arrow struck. San Felipes prided themselves on being able to shoot three shafts into the air before the first one touched the ground. Even as the grizzly charged, another arrow thudded into the bear's shoulder. Bent Willow also fired as the grizzly charged. Before the raging animal could cover the few yards that separated them, his chest and neck were studded with a half-dozen feathered shafts.

The old men in San Felipe Village say that the great bears of the mountains have but one mind. If they think of one thing, they cannot concentrate on another. This young grizzly, feeling the sting of flying missiles within him, stopped to bite at one of the offending sticks that hung from his shoulders. Bearlike, he forgot, for the moment, the two humans. Like a great shaggy dog after a flea, he growled and bit at the arrow. The frail shaft crunched between his teeth. He spat out the fragments, but the pain was still there.

Tony Eagle Tail held one arm out to the side to indicate to Bent Willow that they should be silent for a moment. In pantomime, he motioned quickly toward the other cub grizzly, which was coming up from behind. In three steps, Eagle Tail was bending over the precious rifle. He picked up two cartridges. He laid down his bow and fitted the first shell into the magazine on the side of the gun. The next shell clicked home. Tony reached for the lever. He had never owned a gun, but he had seen Felipe shoot this one a hundred times.

Perhaps it was the metallic click of the rifle mechanism. Tony Eagle Tail never knew. There was a hot breath on his shoulder. Bent Willow's short cry of warning came too late. The bear was on Eagle Tail before he half-raised the gun. In a moment of confusion, he reached also for the bow at his feet. The grizzly struck as he bent over. The slam of the paw knocked Eagle Tail sprawling across Felipe's dead body. Like any brave warrior, Tony Eagle Tail twisted as he lay there and brought the rifle around. But the mechanism of the breach yawned open. No shell was yet in the chamber. The grizzly fell forward upon him as he lay there.

Feebly, he thrust the useless rifle toward the bear. The animal bent over him, biting and raking at the Indian's belly with his claws.

Bent Willow saw Tony's legs protruding from beneath the bear, thrashing and writhing. He turned to run. His mouth was open, and he gasped like a man who is choking to death.

"Shoot!" The shout was frenzied. Bent Willow froze in his flight. "Shoot!" Tony called again. His cry was muffled by the growls of the bear.

Bent Willow turned back to face death. He ran forward. In a few quick steps, he stood at the side of the bear. The animal was chewing at the face of the man beneath him. Bent Willow pulled at his bow until the head of the arrow touched the wood. Even as he did so, Tony Eagle Tail's flailing legs relaxed and were still. Bent Willow released the bowstring at the moment Eagle Tail died.

The snap of the bow and the thud of the shaft in the grizzly's side were one sound. The arrow disappeared in the beast's fur. Only the feathers still showed, slowly staining with red. The bear did not turn but continued to maul the limp body of Tony Eagle Tail.

Bent Willow was already fitting another arrow to the string. From the corner of his eye, he saw movement. It was the fourth bear. This last grizzly was more timid than his litter mates; nevertheless, he advanced. The smell of blood and death was in his nostrils. The mouthings of the bear that had attacked Tony Eagle Tail spoke of food that would be forthcoming.

His eyes on the advancing grizzly, Bent Willow retreated a step or two, holding his bow before him. The odds were now two against one. Both of the grizzlies moved toward Bent Willow. Feathered arrows still protruded from the chest of the one that had killed Eagle Tail.

But it was the deeply buried shaft behind his shoulder that evened the score. The bear seemed dazed at first. He shuffled away from the mauled and bloody carcass that had been Tony Eagle Tail. Drops of blood ran out of the grizzly's nostrils. The bear panted and humped his back as though in pain. Slowly, as if pulled from the side by an invisible cord, he rolled over. Dizzily, he struggled to regain his feet, then fell back, his eyes glazed.

Bent Willow was young, but he had learned the lore of a lifetime in the few minutes there on that canyon ledge. One thing was certain. Arrows would not kill the silver-tipped bears except at close range. Bent Willow reached over his shoulder and brought forth two arrows. They were his last. He shrugged off the strap of the empty quiver, put two arrows between his teeth. With the arrow already on his bowstring, he had three missiles and no more.

So it was that the last of the antagonists advanced, each toward the other. Bent Willow would die as bravely as his friends had. His panic was gone. Even the grizzly seemed to realize there was no turning back. There had been too much blood spilled already, and now it was a fight to the bitter finish.

Bent Willow shot his first arrow into the neck of the grizzly before him. It struck to one side. At the sting of pain in his throat, the bear bent his head and bit off the base of the shaft, then charged forward. Bent Willow had already put another arrow in place. In one motion, he bent the bow and shot. The shaft thudded into the bear's chest.

Bent Willow dropped to one knee as he fitted his last arrow to the string. The bear was above him. Blindly, he pulled the bow to the breaking point. The string snapped. At the same instant, the bow was swept from his hands and he saw the arrow bury its full length under the bear's armpit.

Bent Willow rolled from beneath the grizzly's paw, but too late. The first blow had torn most of the flesh from his upper arm. Holding the wound with his other hand, he rose to his knees and threw himself sideways. The grizzly's teeth snapped an inch away from the bare flesh on his back.

With the speed of a doomed man, he twisted away and struggled to his feet to meet death-face-to-face. The grizzly seemed to slow in his movements. Dazedly, Bent Willow watched doom advance upon him. The bear wrinkled up its lips for the final bite. It never came. Growling low in his throat and mouthing defiance, the grizzly tottered and fell forward at Bent Willow's feet.

The Indian never moved as the bear thrashed and died before him.

The great hunters of San Felipe always tell of how Bent Willow came into the Pueblo late that night. He still held the flap of flesh on his upper arm with one hand. Bent Willow spoke slowly, for he was weak from loss of blood. "We met the strongest in the mountains, but our medicine was greater than theirs. It was four against four."

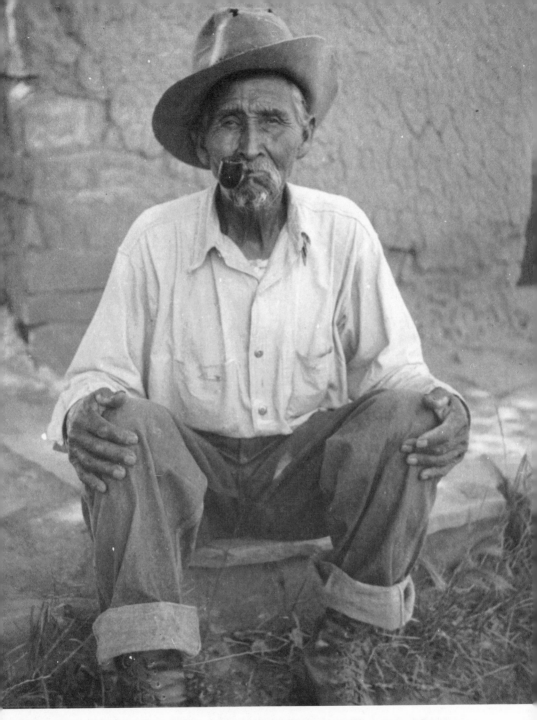

Juan de Dios. Picture taken in 1934 when I rode with Juan de Dios around Dead
Man's Mesa and he told me of the Dead Man's Stampede. Juan was, at that time,
about ninety years old.
Photograph taken by author.

Juan de Dios with a group of Apache scouts. Place unknown but probably near Ft. Union, New Mexico. Juan, himself, is in center with sombrero. Photographer, E.P. Houghton, circa 1870. Photo given to author by Juan de Dios.

Friend of Juan de Dios, Chief Shee-zah-nan-tan, a Jicarilla Apache who took part in the Medio Dia Massacre. Photo taken in 1874 by Timothy H. O'Sullivan probably in Santa Fe, New Mexico in front of the Governor's Palace.

Santigo Largo (James Long), friend of Juan de Dios, who took part in the Medio Dia Massacre. Photo taken in 1888.

Chief Augustine, one of the bowmen at the Medio Dia Massacre. Circa 1890.

Bowman with his squaw and a buffalo skin. Photo taken at Abuquiu Ration Point in 1874.

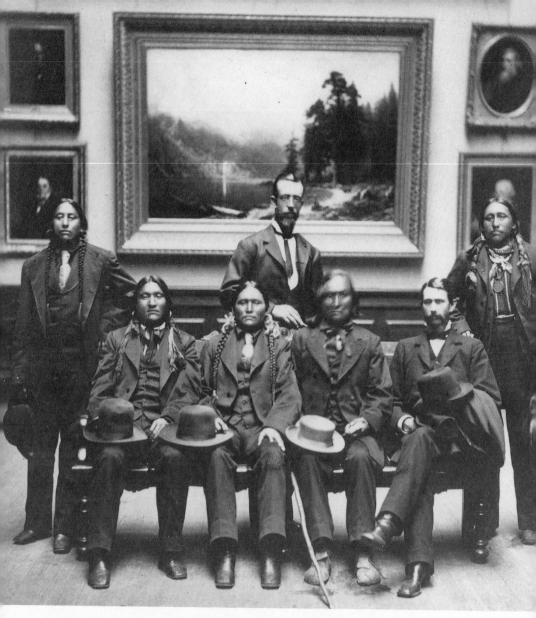

Delegation of Jicarilla Apaches visiting Washington D.C., April 2, 1880. Some of the chiefs in this picture took part in the Medio Dia Massacre.

This illustration, by Bob Kuhn, was published in Field & Stream, April 1962. The author purchased the original from the artist. Juan de Dios is in a spindly tree with the grizzly below.

Chino, Chief of the Jicarillas holding a cap and ball double rifle of about 1870 vintage.

Jicarilla Apache camp.

Jicarilla Apache women at camp.

Jicarilla Apache camp on edge of Staked Plains.

Jicarilla Apache Relay Race.

A Mountain lion at bay. This is a big tom but not the "Big Medicine Lion."

Dogs tree a female in the cliffs. We pulled the dogs off and let her go.

The mountain lion, when pursued by dogs, usually climbs a tree. They are extremely agile and can climb to the top of the tallest pine.

Clell Lee, a famous lion-hunter from Arizona, returns from a hunt with a lion and his dogs. The "Big Medicine Lion" was twice the size of this one and with paws much larger.

Each of the Rio Grande Pueblos have a Hunting Society which dances a Hunting Dance during the winter of each year. This is a Deer Dancer from San Juan Pueblo.

The Hunting Society of each Pueblo dances annually to appease the spirits of the deer and elk they have killed. This is the Deer Dance at San Juan Pueblo.

Big Base Blackie was big all over.

Jicarilla Apache deer hunter pauses for a drink at the Rio Navajo. Circa 1900.

Cass Goodner compares his own hand with the massive paw of Big Base Blackie.

Apache bowman and his squaw water their horses at Rio Navajo. Around 1900.

Mule deer antlers shot by Haddos Martines and Sicily Atole.

"Navajo Dance" at Cochiti Pueblo. The Navajo Dance was performed to ward off enemies from the Pueblo, including the evil spirits of bad bears. In ancient times the Navajo were the main enemies of the Rio Grande Pueblos. Circa 1920.

A big bear with fall fat climbs a tree with difficulty.

One of the Bear People's bears. At left is the late Raymond Meeks, Indian Agent for Cochiti Pueblo. Bear-hunter, Cass Goodner is to the right, author in center.

Cass Goodner and author with another of the "Bear People's" bears. This one was yellowish in color. We found yellow hairs caught in the fence around the corn field.

The Rio Grande Pueblos learned to travel eastward to the Great Plains and hunt the vast herds of buffalo there. Here the members of the Hunting Society of San Juan Pueblo dance the Buffalo Dance to appease the spirits of the buffalo already killed and to bring success in the coming hunt.

Before they acquired guns, the Pueblo hunters used bows and arrows to hunt buffalo. This was a chancy business as the Pueblos had few horses. Here Hunting Society bowmen who are going to take part in the hunt dance to appease the spirits of the buffalo. The pueblo women participate in the dance as it was they that skinned the animals and prepared the meat.

Author with a big Alaskan grizzly he shot in 1967. The grizzly is still common in Alaska and Canada thanks to proper management which includes controlled hunting. However, it has virtually disappeared from the West.

CHIEF BUCK OF STINKING LAKE

CHAPTER IX

Hados Martinez and Sicily Atole stood as motionless as two pine trees. The buck did not yet see them. He was still feeding. His wide-spreading, white-tipped antlers moved up and down among the dry leaves of the oak brush as he nibbled kinnikinnick from the frost-starched hillside. The whole rack was as wide across as the length of the .30-30 rifle Atole held in his hand. The gray body of the deer was heavyset and as large as a horse.

"B-en soh, b-en soh," muttered Atole under his breath. "A chief buck."

"B-en soh," agreed Hados Martinez.

In Apache, b-en soh means "big buck," or "chief buck." The Jicarilla Apaches of north central New Mexico have been hunters since the time their ancestors first came to the Southwest. But in the 1980s, many changes have taken place. The Jacarilla Apaches now own a reservation of over a million acres. Apaches go to modern schools. Hados and Sicily talk English on ordinary occasions and they were hunting at this moment with two very wellworn but serviceable Winchester rifles instead of the bows and arrows of bygone days. But the old times die hard, as the Apaches say. In ceremonial matters, the new ways fight with the old. Hunting, as everyone knows, is a ceremony.

Both Atole and Martinez knew these things, but they believed them to a different degree. Both men had muttered "b-en soh," when they saw the big mule deer buck in the oak brush at the bottom of the canyon. The words meant not only a monster mule deer but also a chief of his kind, with powers far greater than those of an ordinary deer. You can tell a chief deer by the wide spread and thickness of his antlers. The old Apaches believe that a chief deer contains the spirit of a great hunter who died in olden times. A chief deer always has a white face and can disappear at will. A chief deer can show his white face in one place, then, a moment later, appear behind you.

"You shoot!" said Atole in English.

Martinez whispered, "No, you shoot first."

The great deer raised his head and looked straight at the two hunters. The face of the buck was grizzled. The throat patch under his chin was as white as the snow that still lay under the pine trees on the side of the canyon. His eyes were dark, and there were two black spots at the corners of his mouth. He stamped his forefoot as he shook his massive head, and the antlers looked even bigger from the front. His eyes caught glints of morning light. It was the chief buck, perhaps the chief buck of all mule deer everywhere.

"Shoot! Shoot!" muttered Atole.

Both men had their rifles raised and ready. Both men were afraid. Hados shook his head.

Apache custom dictates that only an Apache chief can shoot a chief deer and then only with a bow and arrow. Apache custom also dictates that a hunter be generous with his kill. When a hunter shoots a deer, he must give the buckskin to the man hunting with him. The hide of a chief deer is very valuable and is used only in special ceremonies. Sometimes the neck-skin of a chief deer is made into boots. The feet wearing these moccasins will never grow tired.

Both Hados and Sicily, because neither was a chief in the Apache tribe, were afraid to shoot, and yet both men wanted that hide. Whoever shot first must give it to his friend. At the same time, they feared the magic medicine. They could feel the power of the chief of deer as they stood frozen with indecision.

The chief deer licked his black lips with a darting tongue. Suddenly, he whirled. In two bounds he jumped into a gully in the bottom of the little canyon. The two men could see the rack of antlers moving above the oak brush for a few seconds—and then the pointed tines were gone. Sicily and Hados still stood with their rifles raised. They turned and grinned weakly at each other.

"Bad luck," said Hados in English.

It had all started when Sicily killed a deer the day before. Hados and Sicily had hunted together that time, too. Sicily had seen the young buck first and had shot first. Sicily is the best hunter on the whole reservation. In that fall season already, he had killed fifteen deer. On their reservation, the Indians make their own hunting laws and can shoot as many deer as necessary for meat or ceremonial purposes. But Sicily had lived many years in Dulce, New Mexico, the center of the reservation. At Dulce, one learns white man's ways and forgets the ancient ceremonies of the Apaches, especially in hunting. "It does not matter anymore," Sicily argued. With a Winchester rifle and a pickup truck, old Indian ways seemed silly.

When Sicily killed the small buck, he did not turn its head to the east. He knelt in front of the head to examine the antlers. They were small. The deer was three or four years old. Hados shook his head when he saw this. Out of respect to the Deer Tribe, the head of a dead deer must always be turned to the east, and a hunter must never walk in front of the eyes of a dead deer, or, always after that, deer will see the hunter and he can never make another kill.

In cleaning the deer, Sicily used the white man's way. He stripped off the skin and handed it to Hados as a gift. This was as it should be. He did not swing the skin over the body in the four directions, nor did he take out some of the entrails of the dead deer as an offering to the crow. Any hunter who offers to Crow this way makes a friend of crows and ravens. Crow will fly above and chatter where the deer are. If you do not feed him, Crow will lead the hunter through forests and high ridges where there are no deer. When Sicily cleaned the buck, he did not do any of these things. He did not keep the right and left parts of the deer separate. And he did not hang a strip of entrails on the antlers to honor the spirit of the Deer

121

Chief. Sicily just cleaned the carcass like any white hunter does. He bundled the quarters, two at a time, over his shoulder, slid down the side of the mesa to his pickup truck, and dumped them in.

Hados Martinez lives over near Jim Counselor's Trading Post on Canyon Largo, just off the Apache reservation. But Hados was raised in the old ways. His father told him that a hunter must hunt according to the rules. His grandfather had hunted the same way. Hados shook his head and clicked his tongue in disapproval when he saw Sicily skin and dress the deer all wrong. But it is discourteous to complain about another man's procedure at his own kill.

When Hados and Sicily both waited for the other one to shoot first at b-en soh, it was a joke but a tragedy, too. That big chief deer would be a prize for any man. Was it greed or the gods of the hunt that kept them from shooting? For Hados, it was no accident that they had both stood there with their guns raised and let the buck run away. The Deer Chief was offended.

For many years, the Jicarilla Apaches have saved the skins of big chief bucks and used the antlers of big mule deer for the deer and antelope ceremonies. It was only a few years ago that some of the officers of the state of New Mexico came to realize that in the Jicarilla country grow some of the largest mule deer anywhere in North America. A few big sets of antlers were measured. They astounded everyone with their size, massiveness, and number of points. Fifteen antlers from the Apache reservation were recorded with the Boone and Crockett Club. One set scored near the top in these records. The chief buck Sicily and Hados had seen would be well up in the records anywhere in North America. Never, in all hunting history, have so many big bucks come from a single area.

To the Apache hunters, this all made sense. They knew that many chief bucks lived in the mesas and canyons of their reservation. Among these might be the chief buck of all deer anywhere. But to outside hunters, this was a revelation. Non-Indian hunters are allowed to come into the reservation in small numbers, to hunt on payment of a large fee.

But on the first day of the season, it snowed heavily. The blizzard swept down from the Colorado mountains during the night. By the second day of the season, the visibility was poor and the snow was beginning to stack up in the canyons and mesa tops where some hundreds of non-Indian hunters had made their camps. Some visitors began to pull out. But even with only one day of hunting behind them, the hunters had already scored heavily. Ten massive bucks, all of which would place high in the Boone and Crockett records, were checked by the game wardens as they helped the hunters leave the reservation on the slippery, muddy roads. One tremendous head scored at the top. It was one of the largest mule deer ever killed anywhere. But Sicily Atole knew that there was one chief buck, the chief buck, larger and with more medicine than any other, but he did not find this buck among the other deer.

As the storm broke, Sicily Atole hunted the canyon where he and Hados Martinez had seen the chief deer just above Stinking Lake. Sicily climbed the mesa and crouched on the rimrocks before the winter sun showed weakly through the scudding clouds. A dozen or more other hunters had moved up the canyons below him just at daylight. Some of these men were poor hunters—as Sicily could hear their feet crunching snow and rolling rocks. Deer were moving out ahead of these first hunters. A shot was fired and down below a man shouted. But Sicily did not see the big buck. He had figured that the first few shots would bring the big chief buck out of the canyon where he lived. Because this canyon is almost bare on both sides where it cuts the edge of the mesa, the chief buck would sneak up through the oak brush in the canyon bottom. Big bucks act that way. The only place the buck could escape was at the very head of the canyon through a strip of oak brush and young pine trees. Sicily waited right there, but the chief buck did not come. Once, Sicily thought he heard hooves on the stony ground. Once, also, the crows called down the canyon, scolding at a deer that moved along—but no deer came. Sicily had not fed the crows—they called falsely.

"Had any luck?" a voice inquired. The man who spoke wore a red hat and a red checked jacket. He was a good hunter. He had moved very quietly up the deer trail at the head of the canyon and had spotted Sicily immediately where he stood, silent and still, among the young pine trees.

Sicily hunted all during the snowstorm and the day after, when the leaden clouds, driven by the fitful wind, continued to cover the dry oak leaves with powdered snow. Twice, he tracked big bucks whose sign showed they had walked through the snow only minutes before. Generally, deer do not move far during a heavy snow. In former years, Atole had always killed a deer if he had found tracks this fresh. Falling snow hides a hunter and drowns out sounds and smells. Sicily was sure that one of the tracks he followed was the chief buck of Stinking Lake Mesa. The tracks were big enough, and the tips of the hooves were rounded off from many years of wear. The trail showed where the buck walked around the heads of several small canyons not far from the edge of the mesa.

But the chief deer kept moving. More and more snow covered over the tracks and they seemed older. By late afternoon, Sicily knew he was hours behind the big buck and gave up the hunt.

After the big storm, the few hunters who were left on the reservation had good hunting. Several more big-antlered bucks were checked out through headquarters at Dulce. Game officials measured some of these and figured that the present season, in spite of the blizzard, would produce as many records for the Boone and Crockett Club as the season before. Several of the lucky hunters were Apache Indians—but Sicily Atole was not among these.

Sicily had promised to get a nice fat deer for the widow of his cousin, who was raising two small children and needed meat. He had also promised to bring a deer to his wife's brother, who worked at the sawmill. Most of all, Sicily had promised himself that he would shoot the big chief deer of Stinking Lake Mesa. He would have fat meat for his family, a chief buckskin, and a big set of antlers to show to the Game and Fish people.

During the next five days, Sicily hunted the roughest country north and east of Stinking Lake. During all of that time, he never fired a shot, although he saw several lesser deer. He hunted by the Indian method of tracking and stalking, and he tried the white man's ways of walking along a canyon side to jump a deer and shoot him as he ran. Sicily had shot hundreds of deer by both methods. Undoubtedly, if anyone had asked who was the greatest deer hunter on the Apache reservation, everyone would have said, "Sicily Atole." But Sicily himself did not think so. While other Indians and outside hunters found big bucks, Sicily did not find the chief deer, nor did he find his distinctive tracks in the crusted snow of the Stinking Lake canyons.

Hunting is know-how with some luck thrown in, as any hunter will tell you. Sicily had the know-how of many years of experience, but his luck was gone. To an Apache Indian, good or bad fortune in hunting is attributed to Killer of Enemies or Child of the Water, two deities of the past who taught the Indians how to hunt and the ceremonies and rituals that go with hunting. Sicily's failure to find the big chief deer was not considered strange among the other hunters of Dulce. For some time now, Sicily Atole, as chief game hunter of the tribe, had been taking up white man's ways and ignoring the rituals of the old Apaches. People on the street at Dulce asked, "How can the chief deer allow himself to be seen if Sicily has insulted the Deer Tribe by forgetting the old ways? Why should Crow help Sicily find the chief deer when Sicily never fed Crow at his former kills?" The other Indian hunters all concluded, shaking their heads, that Sicily Atole's luck had run out.

Indian Hunts and Indian Hunters of the Old West

When Sicily had hunted with his grandfather, he had learned to make offerings to Killer of Enemies and Child of the Water. His grandfather had always placed a dead deer's head to the east and never walked in front of it. His grandfather had always hung the entrails of a buck on the right antler and made offerings to the Crow as Child of the Water had done when he was on earth. His grandfather had always prayed early in the morning of a hunt to the Deer Chief to allow some of his tribe to be killed that the Apaches might have meat.

These things were silly, of course. In the old days, his grandfather had used a bow and arrows and had stalked deer with the stuffed head and antlers of a buck tied on his head as a decoy. But with a modern rifle and a pickup truck, who needed the ritual of those bygone days? Sicily began to wonder.

In another day, the deer season on the Apache reservation would be at an end. Most of the other hunters had loaded deer into their cars and driven out. The old snow on the tops of the mesas was crisscrossed with the tracks of the hunters and the furrowed trails of running deer. A great many of those hunters' tracks were Sicily's own. He was almost afraid to go hunting again. His white hunter friends were whispering that, "Sicily has lost his touch." The Indian hunters hinted at more serious and sinister changes.

In the cold dawn of the last day of the hunt, Sicily left his house as usual. He put his gun and a light lunch that his wife had packed in the truck. He took from beneath his coat a buckskin pouch that his grandfather had given him years before. He carried this to the edge of a clump of trees, away from the road, where no one could see. He stamped down a patch of snow large enough so that he could kneel and unwrap the buckskin package. In it was a bit of red ochre. With this powder, Sicily painted a broad stripe of red across both his cheeks and the bridge of his nose. There was, in the package, a dried bundle of deer sinew. This, Sicily placed on top of the snow to the east of where he knelt. Then, facing the rising sun, he called upon the Chief of the Deer Tribe to hear him. The ancient Apache words of the ritual came easily to his lips. He had not forgotten them, ". . . and allow some of your tribe to fall before my arrows." Sicily finished and rose to his feet. He felt strange. Would the Chief Deer listen to a hunter who hunted with a .30-30? Many white hunters had never heard of the Chief Deer, and they were successful. Perhaps, the b-en soh of Stinking Lake Mesa was the Chief Deer himself. These thoughts ran through Sicily's head as he walked back to his pickup. He left the medicine kit of his grandfather spread out on the trampled snow where he had knelt. A raven picked at the remains of a flattened rabbit that a hunter's car had killed on the road. Sicily took out his lunch and extracted a fat meat sandwich. He threw this in the direction of the raven, which flew up into the limbs of a lightning-killed pine tree. "Here, Black One, if I did not feed you before," he said, "I feed you now."

Sicily drove down the frozen road, muttering to himself. He felt a little ashamed and yet confident. He had been through the canyons on the edge of the Stinking Lake Mesa a dozen times in the last several days, and yet this time he was sure he would see the chief deer.

The b-en soh buck was in the oak brush, almost exactly where Hados and Sicily had seen him first. The white-tipped antlers rose and fell as the buck fed on a low clump of mountain mahogany. Sicily turned toward the east and muttered the words that asked forgiveness of the deer for killing him. Sicily raised his rifle, aiming carefully at the broad back of the buck. The deer raised his head, turned, and looked at him. The shot blasted out. The great buck dropped in the snow. He quivered a little and then was still.

Sicily swung the wide antlers around so that the deer's nose faced the east. As he began to skin the massive gray body, he never stepped in front of the eyes. He hung a strip of the entrails on the right horn. Sicily smiled as he did so. Those antlers would be one of the largest sets ever brought out of the Apache reservation. Sicily also tossed strings of fat from the entrails out onto the snow. A raven appeared out of nowhere and began to pick up the pieces. When the skin was off, Sicily carefully swung the hide over the deer body in the four directions.

He knew, of course, that the big buck had come back to his favorite canyon because all the other hunters, with their noise and human smell, had gone. The black raven had nothing to do with his killing of the chief buck. Or did he? The ways of the old Apaches are strange. But who knows what makes hunters' luck? Perhaps a modern rifle and a pickup truck do not change the old ways after all.

THE BEAR THAT WALKED LIKE A MAN

CHAPTER X

Mrs. Bella Twin slogged through melting May snow along the creek banks of the Beaver River in the Swan Hills of Northern Alberta. Sixty-seven hard years in Canada had bent her frame and stiffened her muscles. She was bone-weary, for she had been on the trapline since before daylight. Over one shoulder she carried several rusted traps. In two of them still hung a pair of marten and in another a large male otter. She would have to skin these animals in her little cabin at the end of the trapline, which was still five miles down the wet trail.

Mrs. Twin shifted her load higher on her stooped shoulder. Her buckskin jacket was soaked through. Her moosehide mittens were freezing to the rusty .22 rifle that she carried in her right hand. She sighed heavily. It would be dark and bitter cold long before she reached the cabin. She was getting too old for the trapline.

Suddenly, from in front of her came a snuffling sound.

Bella Twin had been born in a hunting camp at Yellow Knife, the granddaughter of a great hunter in a tribe of famous hunters. In the old days, her grandfather, Chief Standing Bear, had earned a well-deserved reputation for defending his Cree encampment at Buffalo Crossing at the head of the Peace River. As a boy, he had been given the name Big Bear. He was a lad of sturdy build, tall for a Cree, and was afraid of nothing, even as a child. As a young chief, he was leader of a hunting party. Returning to the Cree camp at Buffalo Crossing, the Indians pulled behind them toboggans loaded with much-needed moose meat, for it had been a lean year for the Cree. Suddenly, a huge grizzly stood before them, blocking their way. The bear was taller by half than any of the men who cowered in the sleds. The bear's black muzzle wrinkled in excitement as it smelled the meat—and it bared its teeth. The grizzly was a she-bear, her dried teats stood out from her lean belly where the ribs showed.

She was starving and should be yet hibernating this early in the spring. The Crees, too, were starving. As the bear walked forward, she turned her head toward Big Bear, instinctively picking out the Indian leader.

Big Bear stood his ground. He already had his sinew-backed bow out of its porcupine-quill-decorated case. He slung his quiver aside as the grizzly lunged toward him. Big Bear held two arrows in his teeth and knocked a third on the bowstring, bending the bow to a backward arc. The bear attacked like a towering, fur-covered man. Before the wide-reaching paws could gather Big Bear in, the bow, in quick succession, buried to the feathers three metal-tipped arrows in the bear's chest.

With one blow to the side of the head, the grizzly killed Big Bear. As the other Indians crouched behind the toboggans of meat, the bear staggered to her feet, then fell forward, as they said later, "like a huge man mortally wounded in the chest." They died there together, the bear and the man.

After the fight at Buffalo Crossing, Chief Big Bear became "Chief Standing Bear," and the story became a legend among the Cree.

Bella Twin, whose name Bella He-we-chin means "she who is protected by a bearskin," knew the story well, but she had never seen such a bear—until now! At the snuffling sound, Mrs. Twin looked up. A dark form stood before her. The thing was as massive as a broken-off tree. At the top, well above the level of her head, Mrs. Twin saw red-rimmed eyes and a tongue that slavered over yellow teeth. In the shadow, she could see, at the level of her face, matted fur on a belly. Higher up were two great paws, half-extended. It was a grizzly, a monster of a grizzly, a grizzly such as Mrs. Twin had never seen before.

Mrs. Twin dropped her bunch of traps with a clank behind her. With her teeth, she seized the tip of her moosehide mitten to jerk it off and free her gun hand. Again, the grizzly made the low snuffling sound in his throat.

The gigantic bear dropped forward. He was going to charge. Mrs. Twin gripped the little .22 and called upon her Cree ancestors to help her.

The ancestors of Mrs. Twin had seen such bears a century ago, but few modern people have done so. Actually, the Inland grizzlies (the Plains bears) have supposedly been extinct for over half a century. The Plains grizzly (Ursus arctos) was presumably the largest of all North American grizzlies. Even the Silver-tip grizzly of the Rocky Mountains is a lesser animal, as was the Golden bear of California. But it was not only the size of the Plains grizzly that amazed the early frontiersmen but also the power and the intelligence of these bears that made them the scourge of the Plains. Many frontiersmen reported harrowing experiences with the bears that, one hunter said, "walk like men and think like men." All bears will stand on the hind feet when startled or to have a better look. Only the Plains grizzly attacks standing upright and charging forward like a man. Even pitted against early types of firearms on the frontier, the Plains grizzly was well-nigh invincible. Against the Indian weapons of lance and bow and arrow, Ursus arctos horribilis was a demon that could scarcely be killed.

And yet some of the early Indians did kill the Plains grizzly. When they accomplished this feat, they wore the teeth and claws of the bear as a sign of prowess. (The claws of the Plains grizzly were very long—as much as seven inches on large males.) Such a claw necklace was passed down for generations from father to son. Plains tribes, such as the Sioux, counted the killing of a grizzly equal to the death of ten men. Chieftains of the mound-building people of Ohio traded pearls and copper for the claws and teeth of the great bear of the Plains. These trophies were buried in the tombs of the Mound Builder princes of the Middle West and were rated among their most precious possessions.

Indian Hunts and Indian Hunters of the Old West

The first eyewitness accounts of the great Plains grizzly come from the writings of early explorers, priests, or adventurers, such as Samuel Hearne and Baron de Lahontan, who, in the 1700s, described the great bears that lived in the buffalo prairies and, "fall fiercely upon the huntsmen." In 1805, Lewis and Clarke, met the Plains grizzly in the northern prairies, and in their famous diary, the explorers rated these bears as fiercer and more dangerous than hostile Indians. In this same journal, under May 14, 1805, there is an account of shooting a Plains grizzly. Captain Lewis shot the bear through the lungs. The wounded bear first pursued the hunter who had shot him for half a mile. Then the grizzly retreated a mile, dug a great hole in the wet earth, and covered his bleeding chest with mud to plug the wound.

Early accounts indicate that the main food of Ursus arctos horribilis was buffalo. An eyewitness account of a Plains grizzly at his deadly work was given by an Indian named Juan de Dios, who died in 1936. As a young man, Juan had made part of his living hunting antelope and mountain sheep along the Purgatoire River and supplying the wagon trains going over Raton Pass to Santa Fe with meat. Although it was dangerous because of the warlike Kiowa and Cheyenne, Juan and his band of Apaches made several forays to hunt buffalo in the northern plains along the Missouri.

On one of these trips, they saw a great bear with a hump on his shoulders, holding his head low. It was a grizzly, but not such a grizzly as the Apaches had seen in their native mountains of New Mexico. This bear seemed to roll along over the prairie grass, as big as a buffalo himself. As Juan and his men watched, the bear stalked up a coulee and began to crouch low, like a coyote trying to catch a rabbit. The Indians could see, at the head of the coulee, a small herd of buffalo. They were all bachelor bulls. Some of the buffalo were feeding and some were standing in the morning sun. As the bear approached the bulls, he crouched low so that only his hump showed above the prairie grass. Even at that distance, Juan could see the sunlight ripple on the silver-tipped hairs of the grizzly as he hunched himself forward on his belly. One of the buffalo turned to look at the thing moving toward them. The hump was no farther from them than a fair rifle shot. Other buffalo turned to stare. One of them threw up his head in alarm. With a roar, the grizzly lunged to his feet and charged. In arching bounds he closed the distance. The bulls turned to run. The grizzly reared up like a gigantic man. He raised a paw and smashed it down on the skull of one bull, just behind the horns. Another bull turned. It lowered its head to hook a horn into the bear's belly. Again the grizzly's paw swung down. The buffalo dropped with its skull crushed. The other bulls ran off as the grizzly stood on his hind feet to watch them go. The bear dropped on the carcass of one of the two bulls, bit out mouthfuls of hair and hide, and spit them out. Then he began to feed, starting on the belly.

From a few other early accounts such as that of Juan de Dios, it is obvious that the Plains grizzly was mostly a meat-eater and that he had little difficulty in stalking and killing his prey. But when the buffalo were killed, first by meat hunters such as Juan de Dios and then by hide hunters in the 1880s, the Plains bears were left without their main food supply. There were other factors that hastened their extinction. The grizzly of the Plains was no shrinking violet. As Lewis and Clarke had found, to their sorrow, early in the century, the Plains grizzly seldom turned aside when he saw a human. A wagon pulled by horses was fair game and the horses a substitute for the buffalo that were gone. The last great buffalo hunts, from 1870 to 1875, were staged by the hunters who collected buffalo hides and left the meat to rot. When the last bison herds disappeared before the Sharps rifles of the hide hunters, the market for buffalo robes was still an active one in the eastern United States and Europe. Some of the head hunters turned to Plains grizzlies in their quest for beautiful long-furred robes that might bring ten dollars on the New York market. A few of the robe hunters went to Alaska and began to hunt Kodiak bear to supply the demands of the easterners for carriage robes and bedspreads. One last great bison-hide hunt took place in 1884. When the hide hunters and skinners returned in 1885, the buffalo herds had vanished. For all practical purposes, the bison were extinct and the Great Plains grizzly with them.

But it was the cattlemen who killed the last of the Plains grizzlies. As the trail herds rolled out of Texas and up the Chisholm Trail or the Goodnight Trail or through the Indian nations and on to the northern grasslands, the last of the Plains grizzlies saw the longhorn cattle as a substitute for buffalo.

One account tells of a trail herd driving through eastern Montana in 1887. In one night, twenty steers were lost to a single bear. The next day, after the cowboys had gathered the terrified and demoralized remaining steers, they drove the cattle toward the ford of a small creek. On the far side of the creek, a grizzly, apparently the same bear that had slaughtered the steers the night before, reared up to challenge them. As the first of the cattle entered the water of the ford, the grizzly advanced into the creek to attack. A lone cowboy emptied his Colt .44 at point-blank range into the bear. Horse and rider went down under the sweep of the grizzly's paw. In a hail of bullets, threshing horses, and stampeding cattle, the bear stood in the bloody waters and fought like a man. Mortally wounded by twenty or thirty slugs in his chest, the bear advanced and fell facedown, like a man, at the last.

In one of the last recorded encounters, a great bear attacked a herd of steers and twenty mounted men on the Goodnight Trail as they crossed the Ute creek in eastern New Mexico. The grizzly stood up, took four slugs from a six-gun in his chest, then killed a horse with one sideswipe of his massive paw. As the other cowboys closed in, the bear knocked two horses and riders sprawling, then collapsed in a furrow of cattle, horses, and bear in a bloody melee. "Bo Jingle," the trail boss of the herd of longhorns, said afterward, "That there bear was as big as a bull and had as much power as a steam engine with the boiler busted."

But scattered remnants of buffalo survived in Yellowstone Park and in a few isolated groups in the northern peripheries of the Great Plains in central Alberta and the northern fringes of central Canada. A few bears that "walk like a man and think like a man" apparently survived also.

Perhaps there were, among these truculent monsters, a few who combined sagacity with bravado. As the buffalo prairies became wheat fields and roads and houses covered their former domain, a few of the bears moved farther north into the Arctic fringes of the northern plains where the wood buffalo was still wild and where humans had not yet penetrated. The northern periphery of the Great Plains is too cold for most agriculture and too remote for most cattle ranchers. There the Plains grizzlies found sanctuary.

Perhaps the first to suspect that the Plains grizzly might not be extinct was Reinhold Eben-Ebenau, a hunter and guide of the Slave Lake region. From the Indian hunters, he had heard stories of grizzlies in the Swan Hills just south of Lesser Slave Lake. The Indians said that these bears were different from other grizzlies. They were of monstrous size and often killed wood buffalo and moose. If a hunter approached one of these bears, the grizzly stood on his hind feet like a giant man.

A naturalist who runs a game farm in northern Alberta, Al Oeming, examined the skull of one of the Swan Hill grizzlies. Swan Hill grizzly skulls were distinctive, as were the descriptions of the appearance and habits of the bears. Oeming went into the Swan Hills to see if, by some chance, a remnant of the Plains grizzlies might still live there. But it was not until Mrs. Bella Twin pushed her trapline deep into the Swan Hills that the question was answered.

Mrs. Twin met the grizzly face-to-face. Juan de Dios and his Apache hunters had been afraid to attack a Plains grizzly with their Sharps buffalo rifles. Mrs. Twin held in her mittened hand the rusty .22 rifle of ancient vintage that she generally used to dispatch small animals caught in her traps. But the Cree Indians come from a long line of hunters. Mrs. Twin did not hesitate as she jerked off her mitten and raised her little gun. As the grizzly stood before her, he seemed to tower twice her height in the gloom of the trail. She pointed her rifle upward, sighted between the reddish eyes, and jerked the trigger. The little bullet furrowed the skin at the base of the bear's nose. He shook his head and fell forward. One huge paw was raised to strike. Mrs. Twin pumped the mechanism of the .22. It was fouled and often didn't work, and the spent shell usually stuck in the ejector. This time, the slide jammed home. She pointed the barrel at the bear's head and again jerked the trigger. Dancing backward, she pumped another shell into the chamber and pulled the trigger. As the bear fell forward, she tripped over the bundle of traps she had dropped on the trail. Still, she jerked the slide of the .22, pressed the muzzle against the bear's head and fired. The grizzly twisted his jaws to find a purchase. Mrs. Twin had one more .22 shell. Again, she called upon her Cree ancestors. The bear's slavering jaws were in her lap. She was finished. The weight of the bear's head was pressing her into the mud. She fired—her last rimfire cartridge, strong enough, perhaps, for a mink or a martin but to pierce the skull of a grizzly who killed buffalo—. Her life hung in the balance. The great slavering head on Mrs. Twin's lap grew heavier. It was six hours later that she reached the trapline cabin, and two days later that she had her broken hip fixed at the hospital at Edmonton.

The government of Alberta was delighted with the prospect of rescuing from oblivion one of the most colorful of North American animals and has declared a ten-thousand-square-mile area of the

Swan Hills a sanctuary for grizzly bears. Although these last of the Plains grizzlies have turned from killing the Plains buffalo of former years to killing and eating occasional wood buffalo and moose, the Alberta government considers the loss of game well worth it. Now a modern man, if he is hardy and if he is lucky, can go into the "Valley of the Giants" and see the grizzled bear that "walks like a man and thinks like a man."

BEAR PEOPLE'S BEAR

CHAPTER XI

T he circle of Indians stood before us, silent and waiting. Cass Goodner pushed his flat-topped sombrero to the back of his head and scratched above one eye reflectively. "If it's so all-fired important," Cass said, as though to himself, "I don't see why you Injuns don't catch him yourself."

One impassive man, Pablo Sanchez by name, stood a little forward, as if he accepted the leadership of the rest of the men. Although he wore the rough trousers and soft-skinned moccasins of all the Cochiti Indians, he also had on an elaborate embroidered shirt, which clearly indicated that he regarded this as a special occasion and no ordinary, workaday conference. Pablo shook his head sadly from side to side, and the bright cerise band of ribbon that he wore around his temples caught the glint of the early morning sun. His eyes were troubled, as though he felt that his long explanation had been for nothing.

But Cass Goodner knew the story as well as Pablo Sanchez himself. Cass had lived for many years in the country of Pueblo Indians and perhaps knew their ways and customs better than any other rancher on the edge of the Rio Grande Valley. "Yeah, I know," he said quietly in response to Pablo's elaborate shrug. "It's the Bear People again."

As I looked around at the grim faces of the Indians before us, I remembered the story. One of these very men had told it to me when we sat around a campfire of a hunt several years before.

There had lived, in the pueblo of Cochiti, on the banks of the Rio Grande, a young girl. That was many years ago, before the Americans came with their covered wagons, even before the Spaniards came. This young girl of Cochiti was too proud to marry among the Pueblo people, so she went into the mountains and there met a Bear. The Bear was big and strong, with large teeth and powerful paws. He took the girl back to his cave. She married the Bear and lived in his cave, and they raised a family of many children. So strong is the medicine of all bears that the children of this marriage were like bears themselves. They inherited from the Cochiti girl only the cunning of the Indian hunters. In all other ways they were like bears. In the years after the Cochiti girl raised her bear family, these Bear People came close to the pueblo many times. Especially did the Bear Children come down in the fall to eat the ripened corn in the fields above Cochiti village. The Bear People were careful, in those days, to eat only the corn that belonged to the family of the girl.

The Bear People came year after year to eat corn. Usually, the Cochiti planted special fields for the Bear People's convenience. In all this time there had been no trouble.

"Now," Pablo Sanchez had told us in his grave manner, "the Bear People tear down the stalks even in the valley fields. They destroy the corn of all the clans of Cochiti."

Cass and I understood well the point that Pablo Sanchez was making. The Bear People were despoiling the food supply of all the people of Cochiti. This was not only a disaster but unjust as well; it had been only the family of the girl who deserved these reprisals. It mattered little that the girl had married the Bear many centuries ago. Of course, these Indians could not kill the Bear People or they would be making war against relatives of their own people. Added to the difficulty of the Bear People's being actual relatives, there was the danger of the medicine inherent in all bears. The Indians of all the pueblos of the Rio Grande have a wholesome respect for this bear medicine. They will not even step in a bear's tracks if they can possibly avoid it.

But with Cass Goodner, it was different. This blue-eyed rancher with the affable manner had helped these Indians in a hundred ways in the past. He spoke for them in government matters, helped them find their lost cattle, and was sympathetic when Indian ways conflicted with the encroaching American civilization round about. Now the delegation with Pablo Sanchez wanted Cass to help them with the corn-eating bears.

Cass Goodner went with Pablo Sanchez to view the damage that the Bear People had done. I suspected that Cass wanted to see the tracks in the dirt of the field to find how many bears were involved and how big they were. Both Cass and I knew that the acorn crop in the mountains behind Cochiti Pueblo had been a complete failure that year. Bears had already made their appearance in several incongruous places. They had rifled the garbage cans of the atomic town of Los Alamos, to the north of Cochiti. Bears had even come down out of the mountains and eaten grapes in vineyards close to Albuquerque, where no bears should be. But Cass said none of these things to his Indian friends. He merely nodded gravely to Pablo Sanchez as the Indian pointed out the one cornfield that was damaged the most.

Even from a distance, it looked as though a truck had driven through the corn patch. The stalks were bent down at all angles. Here and there, the green ears had been bitten through, husks and all. Most of the destruction, however, was purely wanton.

Cass circled the fresh earth at the edge of the field. "All seems to be one bear—here anyhow," he muttered, half to himself. Then he pointed to the fence at the upper edge of the corn patch. "Look there!"

Here the Indians had strung a number of additional strands of barbed wire in an abortive attempt to keep out the Bear People. A gaping hole had been torn through the fence. The bear had surged against three or four of the strands and broken them like cotton string. Cass plucked a tuft of light-colored hairs from a barb on a railing piece of wire and handed it to me. The long hairs were the color of corn itself. A yellow bear!

Indian Hunts and Indian Hunters of the Old West

I knew even before Cass climbed into his pickup truck to get his hound pack that he was going to hunt the corn-eating bears, and it wasn't just to help his Indian friends. Any fresh bear track or lion kill would start Cass Goodner off on a hunt, even though it might be the middle of branding season on his ranch. As it was, we had planned to go on a September bear hunt, anyhow, and had been uncertain what direction to take because of the lack of acorns in the mountains.

We did not let the dogs out of the truck near the cornfields but drove as far as we could into the foothills of the mountains behind the pueblo. There was a small woods road that led up to the mouth of Peralta Canyon directly behind Cochiti. With our two horses in a trailer we negotiated this difficult track as far as the box canyon of Peralta. Cass had come here for a definite purpose.

In the middle course, Peralta Canyon comes together like the narrow mouth of a funnel. Here the smooth lava walls of rock are so narrow that a horseman, threading through this difficult place, can reach out and touch the walls on either side. At the very top of this narrow defile, the canyon cliffs actually overlap, shutting out the light from above.

This is the place called the Bear Jump by the Cochiti Indians. The way in which the Bear Jump got its name is another story that has little to do with the Bear People and their raids on the cornfields. The narrow confines of the Bear Jump is a natural pass for all animals moving to and from the mountains. There are also occasional pools of water along the floor of the canyon where a bear might slake his thirst after a hot night chewing on corn in the fields near the pueblo.

Even before we unloaded the horses from the trailer, Cass leaned out of the cab of his truck and glanced significantly at the first pool of water at the very mouth of the Bear Jump box. The water was muddy, and the margins of the puddle were marked and trampled. A bear had not only drunk at the spot the night before but had also wallowed in the water.

We made our camp by the Bear Jump at the mouth of a cave that had been lived in by Indian cliff dwellers many centuries ago. Before daylight the following morning, we were on fresh bear sign. Our dogs were anxious and so were our horses. We started the track at the edge of the water below Bear Jump box.

That evening, we dragged back into camp on our jaded mounts with the dogs trailing behind in a dejected file of lowered heads and drooping tails. We had followed a set of bear tracks that led down out of the mountains, around the edges of the cornfields, and back into the mountains again without jumping any bear. Cass expressed it very well as he stepped stiffly down from his horse and remarked, "We might just as well have stayed in camp."

Although we did not actually run the yellow bear that first day, apparently he knew that hounds and men were after him. He did not go down again to the cornfields and the open country near the pueblo. Perhaps, with the cunning that had been imparted to his ancestors, according to the Indian story of the bear-human marriage, this particular animal knew the ways of men. Cass had boasted that if we caught the yellow bear in the flats below the foothills, he would, "rope him and tie him like a three-legged steer." At any rate, from that time on the yellow bear took to the rough country toward the head of Peralta Canyon.

In that jumbled region, the rocks are volcanic. The canyons are lined with tufts and lavas in various layers that erode straight-sided and precipitous. Even the side canyons are crumpled and impassable. In many places it is impossible for a man, or even a dog, to climb or descend these canyon walls for several miles.

Along the remote ledges of the canyon, the yellow bear left behind him innumerable tracks. We found these traces days later, or, at the least, hours after the bear had passed that way. During these difficult times, the yellow bear ate raw apples as a substitute for Indian corn. He also grew thinner and, therefore, harder to catch.

On the grueling rides that we made in pursuit of the yellow bear in the Peralta Canyon country, we learned much about his habits. For one thing, he would not climb a tree. The yellow bear was, of course, a black bear in a yellow color phase. Many of the black bears of the Jemez Mountain region are not always black but are often brown, or, rarely, yellow like this one. The black bears can, and often do, climb a tree, especially when hard-pressed by a pack of snarling hounds. But the yellow bear of Peralta Canyon did not, although we jumped him several times and even got a glimpse of him once. His technique when closely pursued was to go through the roughest and most broken country. There were occasional cracks in the lava rimrock, hidden by close-growing bushes or stunted trees. On several occasions, the yellow bear made good his escape through such places, which only he seemed to know.

The general trend of the conversation in Cochiti Pueblo during that fall hunt was that Cass Goodner was hunting the chief of the Bear People. Other bears of less interesting personality and color continued to raid the Cochiti cornfields until the crop was harvested, when they returned to the mountains. The Indians understood Cass's growing obsession to catch the one important bear. Several times, the Indians visited us at our camp near the Bear Jump. They listened with understanding to our stories of difficult chases, of horses falling in the rocks, and dogs cut off on precipitous ledges.

"The chief of the Bear People is wise in the ways of men," Pablo Sanchez told us one evening as he sat before our fire. "You will never catch him."

Pablo Sanchez came very close to being right. We did not catch the yellow bear that first fall. I thought, myself, that we needed some special medicine to overcome the great power of the yellow bear. I had hunted with the Indians long enough to believe that it is medicine of this kind that makes the difference between success and failure. Several people call it hunter's luck. The Indians know better. That winter, in the kiva ceremonials at Cochiti Pueblo, the medicine societies concocted powerful ceremonies against the Bear People.

The following year, the bear season in New Mexico began on September 15. The acorn crop in the Peralta Canyon country was scattered, but there were plenty of chokecherries and raw apples. Raymond Meeks, an employee of the Indian Service, accompanied us on the hunt as the representative of the pueblo. Raymond had ridden his whole life in the Cochiti country and knew every little hidden trail and talus slope by which we could get up or down a difficult place. Pablo Sanchez suggested that we had better paint our faces with a strip of vermilion color across the bridge of the nose. The Indians always hunt with their faces painted in that way. Cass and I thought it unnecessary, however, since our faces would soon be black from campfire smoke, anyway.

On the first day of that hunt, we circled wide to cut for sign. Below the Bear Jump, two or three small bears had wandered out of the foothills down toward the pueblo, but none had the broad, flat track of the yellow bear. Toward the head of Peralta Canyon, we came across old tracks along the canyon floor that were undoubtedly those of the chief of the Bear People. The acorns were scattered, however, and we found no place where the yellow bear had stayed long or fed for more than a single day.

"There's a hidden canyon up here a few miles," Raymond Meeks happened to remark that evening as we unsaddled the horses. "There's a spring there too, and an old cabin."

Cass showed quick interest. "I know the place. I saw it from the top of the cliff, but there's no way a man can get a horse in there."

Raymond nodded vigorously. "There's a trail right into the place. There's a mine there too with a streak of silver rock as wide as your hand. The Indians killed the miners in 1899. Hardly anybody's been there since."

I knew before we started the next morning that we would head toward the hidden canyon, if only to see the old silver mine. The water there sounded like a good bet, also. Bears drink every day after they feed, especially if they are eating bitter acorns with lots of tannic acid in them.

Raymond Meeks led the way. Halfway up the length of Peralta Canyon, he paused by an old prospecting hole. "This looks like the place," he mumbled to himself. He forced his horse through a heavy growth of young pines to one side of the canyon. A small gully opened up before us. We could make out a faint trail, long overgrown. There were stumps of dead trees on either hand that had been cut long ago for mine stopping. Here and there along the old trail, clumps of raw apples hung from lush green thickets. Bears had been feeding on them, for there were torn branches with withered leaves on the ground.

But the yellow bear had not been there—at least not recently. The hounds sniffed eagerly at the places where the bears had pulled down the thorny raw branches to strip away the red fruit into their mouths. Sissy, our female strike dog, more than once pointed her muzzle into the gentle wind that drifted down out of the hidden canyon. Sissy's eyes showed interest; her tail wagged tentatively, but she did not bark.

As we moved forward up the faint trail, the other dogs, too, were increasingly active. They moved ahead of us as we forced our horses through the thick-growing brush that choked the narrow entrance to the canyon. In half a mile, the rock walls opened out on either side. The place was as large as four or five city blocks. Yellow pines and Douglas fir grew in open-spaced clumps with parklike vistas in between. Over the tops of these trees, we could see the straight-sided cliffs that cut off this secluded place from the rest of the mountain world.

Cass and I glanced at each other and grinned. Just then Sissy barked up ahead, sharp and insistent. In another instant, all the hounds bayed at once. It was not the barking of dogs that have found a fresh track. The hound pack was looking at something.

"Could be a badger," said Raymond.

Cass shook his head. A new chorus of barking broke out in front of us. We spurred our horses forward, and the hounds moved away at the same time. The dogs were barking and running.

As we rounded a clump of pines at a full gallop, we saw before us an old cabin. I caught a glimpse of a roughly made stone chimney at one end and a sagging porch. In front of the cabin was a small depression. In this was the glint of running water. Lush aquatic plants grew along the sides. The water was still roiled when we galloped through it. I did not need to hear Cass shout from ahead, "Come on, they've jumped him!"

The roar of the dogs now echoed off the cliff walls before us. With echoes and counter-echoes, the sounds became confusing. Both Cass and Raymond Meeks were spurring their horses through the dense brush on the far side of the cabin clearing with the reckless abandon of men who did this every day of their lives. My own mount was a skittish animal. He balked when we suddenly came upon a pine snag hidden in the tall grass. It took precious seconds to find a way around this obstacle. No longer could I see the plunging forms of men and horses ahead. I could only hear Cass's voice drifting back through the tumult of the dogs. "We've got him trapped against the cliff."

From my position farther back, it seemed that the sounds of the chase were swinging over to the right to make a circuit of the little canyon and the cabin at its center. I had fallen badly behind and was now cut off by a solid mass of raw apples. In a bear chase, even split seconds are precious. Cass and I had found out before that even if we rode at breakneck speed, the yellow bear usually outran us. I spurred my horse viciously and swung low to avoid the raking thorns of the haws. The horse kept swinging to the right, seeking openings through the brush.

For a minute or two, we ran free down a trail that seemed to lead from the old cabin to a mine shaft. With my head bent low, I saw an old, rusty shovel lying by the trail as I galloped past. Suddenly, the sounds of the dogs were just ahead. My horse had been cutting across the canyon. The hounds had swung the bear in a half-circle and were heading for the entrance to the canyon.

Reaching down, I loosened the rifle in the scabbard beneath my right leg. I looked up only once and saw the lava cliffs close ahead. There was an open place at the very foot of the rock with two or three scattered pines of large size.

In that instant, my horse braced his front feet and slid to a jolting stop. The maneuver caught me unprepared. The momentum shot me forward, half out of the saddle, and I grasped the neck of the animal like any jockey unseated after a disastrous jump. I had lost one stirrup, anyway, so I slid down on the wrong side of the horse. It was then that I saw the horse's ears. They were pricked forward like two pointers. He had flared out his nostrils as horses do when they are badly frightened. I looked past his nose. There was the bole of a yellow pine, perhaps three feet through. I became aware that the noise of the dogs was deafening and close, although I could not see them. Perhaps that had scared this damnable horse.

Thinking I had better go it on foot or the crazy animal would kill me, I reached to slip the rifle out of its scabbard. The horse whirled. The gun stuck in the leather, and I was almost jerked off my feet, but it came free. When I turned around, I was face to face with the yellow bear!

The animal clung to the far side of the bole of the yellow pine, with his buttocks at the height of my head. My horse had galloped straight into him, and he had hopped up on this refuge on the spur of the moment. He stuck his head around the tree and looked at me, but the chief of the Bear People was not a tree-climbing bear. Even as I stared in that first instant, he shifted his paws downward. His broad head with the yellow-rimmed ears turned. I was so close that I could see the wet brown nose and the half-opened jaws beneath as he panted after his run. A drip of stringy saliva dribbled down onto the yellow fur of his chest.

Cass was yelling something in the background. I heard Raymond answer off to one side. One of the hounds burst through a screen of bushes on the far side of the tree. The bear looked around at the dog, then shifted his hind feet lower. One paw touched the ground. I raised the rifle and fired quickly. A puff of yellow fur spurted out on the bear's shoulder. He turned his head toward me and his eyes met mine as I stood there. They were intelligent eyes. There seemed to be no anger in them—only a question. The bear bent forward to bite the wound in his shoulder. Then, all at once, the big head dropped sideways. His hind legs crumpled. The loose body dropped heavily to the ground and rolled a little down the slope. Then the hounds came to worry the carcass.

Cass, Raymond, and I were congratulating each other. "Guess those Injuns will be glad this yellow bear is dead," Cass commented.

"I'm not so sure," I said, as I lifted one heavy paw. "I think they'll miss the chief of the Bear People."

Perhaps they did, too, for it was only a few days later that a delegation of Indians came to see us. They would like, they said, the tail of the yellow bear to use as a talisman. Even a piece of the body of the chief of the Bear People would be the most powerful medicine in Cochiti.

GHOST ELK

CHAPTER XII

We waited for Santiago Yepa to speak. Our wrinkled friend who sat across the fire was no ordinary Indian. It is true that he was war chief among the Jemez tribe of New Mexico, but this was a mundane office in itself. It was rumored that Santiago was also in league with the spirits. But on this occasion, we were asking for Santiago's advice in neither of these capacities. We had inquired about his knowledge of the elk that lived on San Antonio Mountain.

"Sure bet no good," Santiago answered tersely and nodded his head up and down with absolute finality as he spoke.

The firelight played on his bronze features, and the radiating lines around his mouth showed dark as we looked at him. The black eyes of the Indian were sunk deep in his time-creased cheeks. The yellow light from the small campfire reflected on those eyes, and there was an illumination that seemed to shine from them, as though the fire came from inside.

"You mean to say that there aren't any elk on San Antonio Mountain?" Bill Burk protested. "Why, I myself saw hundreds."

Santiago stopped him with an upraised hand. Even this gesture seemed somehow regal, although Santiago himself was plain enough in his Indian way. The hair at the nape of his neck was gathered in a double bun, looped over with a strip of red cloth. His buckskin leggings were dirty and frayed in places. Some of the silver buttons that looped up the side of his high moccasins were missing. Santiago's shirt was of plain cotton cloth like that of any other Indian and so faded that the uncertain light of the fire scarcely picked out any of the gay plaids with which it had once been decorated.

"But these elk—different. They go away. So!" Santiago flipped a small coal from the edge of our campfire out into the darkness

151

beyond. The tiny red thing glowed for a moment and then went out. Bill Burk and I looked in fascination at this physical display of the mysteries of San Antonio Mountain. When we turned to question Santiago further, he was gone.

"He gives me the creeps," Bill said. "How that Indian can slide in and out of these shadows is beyond me. He talks of ghosts, but he's one himself."

We were already committed to the hunt on San Antonio Mountain. We knew that the place was sacred to the Indians, and we also knew that there were elk there. Since this particular herd had never been hunted in modern times, we were certain of getting a magnificent trophy head. It was in this regard that we had questioned Santiago Yepa about the sacred mountain and the elk herd that lived there. After all, this was his territory, even though San Antonio Mountain was far from Jemez lands.

San Antonio Mountain was no ordinary peak. Originally, the place had been a volcano, and in geological times of antiquity, the troubled skin of the earth had erupted here to throw up heaps of crumbling ash and pour out streams of molten stuff through this cosmic wound. But these terrible events had occurred long ago, and the quiet of the wild had settled long since over the mountain. Gradually, the place had been clothed by forest trees. The moisture on the summit of the volcano was enough to bring forth groves of aspens and clinging oak brush. But the conical shape of San Antonio Mountain still betokened its volcanic origin, as Bill and I looked up at its dark bulk against the lighter shades of the night sky beyond our fire.

"I still don't see how we can miss," Bill Burk was saying. "It's an isolated mountain, and we know that the elk are there. If they're not on one side, they'll be on the other."

There was irrefutable logic in what Bill said. If we didn't find one of those gigantic bull elk on one side of the ancient volcano, we would find one on the other. There were supposed to be three hundred of the animals somewhere up there in the darkness on those volcanic slopes, and we knew, also, that some of those animals carried on their heavyset necks racks of antlers that would set off any living-room fireplace with a magnificent display. But still the words of Santiago Yepa came back to us as we turned into our sleeping bags, "Sure bet no good."

San Antonio and a twin volcano, Ute Mountain, rise a thousand feet above a vast, open series of plains west of the Rio Grande Gorge, close to the New Mexico—Colorado state line. These sagebrush and bunchgrass plains are, perhaps, ten miles across. The two mountains stand out, as Bill Burk said, "like two prunes in a glass of buttermilk." The elk herd of San Antonio and the few deer of Ute Mountain would never cross the miles of open grassland between them and any other place, for that matter. The elk were trapped by their own isolation.

We took Santiago Yepa along for two reasons. For one thing, he was a famous tracker and hunter and had been to both San Antonio and Ute mountains many times in the past years. For another, I knew that the Jemez tribe had a sacred shrine on San Antonio, where, annually, they place green fir boughs and prayer plumes (painted stakes with special feathers and fetishes tied to the tips), and I knew why the Jemez tribe left offerings at a shrine so far from their town of Jemez on the Jemez River, forty miles to the south. I knew, too, the reason that the Jemez tribe would travel so far to show respect for the "Cloud People," but that story of long ago is not a part of this narrative. Also, I knew that San Antonio, being a sacred mountain to Santiago and his tribe, should be treated as hallowed ground. I did not want to violate this without Santiago's permission. He and his family were my old friends.

The next morning, we finished our coffee just as the winter constellation of Orion was tipping downward toward the horizon. In the east, the sky showed a luminous band, and against the gathering light, we could see the bare outline of the pine trees on the lower slopes around us. Somewhere up in the darkness of the mountain, a jay twittered with a discordant note. The elk season, for us, had begun on San Antonio Mountain.

Officially, the season had begun at noon of the previous day, for the New Mexico Game Department, in its wisdom, had decreed that this hunting season, like many others, would commence when the sun stood at its zenith and all good elk were asleep. There were a few other hunters in this isolated place who had camped on the opposite side of the mountain and would mount the volcanic ridges from that direction. But that was good, we thought. Any animals that those hunters might encounter would inevitably be driven in our direction and make our choice of the mightiest racks of antlers on San Antonio Mountain easier.

Volcanic terrain is different from other places. At first blush, it seems barren, and much of the ground is naked of grass covering. Ash surfaces are studded with rounded stones of pumice and lava that dropped there during the eruption of long ago. These rolling pieces underfoot are a constant menace, and there is no spot in all these slopes where a climber can put his foot down flat on the surface of the ground.

In spite of the treacherous footing and the rough nature of the ridges, there is a richness in volcanic earth that gives the mountain a character all its own. Perhaps these materials spewed up from the very soul of the planet itself carry in their makeup minerals and richness that do not occur in ordinary soils. The pine trees grow thicker, even from the seemingly sterile ash, and the aspens and the oaks are sturdy and verdant as they suck their sustenance from the rich minerals amid the cinders.

The animals, too, that live in such places seem sturdier and heavier for these same reasons. We had seen one or two elk antlers, shedders from some seasons past, that the Indians had brought from

154

San Antonio Mountain. They were gigantic horns of their kind, and the beams where the antlers had emerged from the bull's head were of a circumference that could hardly be spanned by the combined fingers of a large man's hands. It was antlers such as these that Bill and I envisioned as we mounted the difficult slops of the mountain on that morning.

Santiago had told us that the elk of San Antonio habitually lived on the very peak of the mountain. Even in the winter this was so, and they retreated from their summit sanctuary only when forced to do so by the deepness of the snow that covered their food supply. As it was, there was little snow, and we knew the elk would be high.

On the very summit of San Antonio was the crater of the volcano. It was no longer a cupped depression complete within itself, such as one thinks of in connection with orthodox volcanoes. This crater had blown out its side in one of the last of the fitful upheavals that had marked its history. Instead of a complete basin, the place was an amphitheater, open to the east and with a canyon running out at its lower edge to mark the spot where the last lava had been spilled in that direction.

This whole semicircular place was, perhaps, a mile across and contained the only moisture on the whole mountain. Here, some small catch basins trapped the trickling waters that ran from the side of the old crater and impounded them in unimposing pools amid the ash and dark sand. Here, too, the elk herd of San Antonio watered when they had finished their feeding for the night. A natural spot for an easy hunt and the real reason we were certain that the San Antonio elk were a sure pushover.

We stood breathing for a moment as we approached the open-sided crater from its lower edge. Checking our guns carefully, we made ready to mount the last few yards of the slope so that the whole amphitheater would be open to view. We had no doubt that at least a hundred elk would be there feeding on the bunch grass.

"Now, don't take the first set of horns that you see," Bill admonished between labored gulps of air. "Remember, there are some museum heads on this mountain, and that's what we came for."

I nodded understandingly as I quieted my breathing from the climb up the slope. We would be calm and pick our animals carefully from the herd in the crater basin.

So Bill Burk and I cleaned the eyepieces on our binoculars and carefully stepped up over the sloping rim of the crater on top of San Antonio Mountain. Santiago Yepa crouched behind us. He had an eerie habit of appearing and disappearing like a ghost. The sun at our back was already throwing the long shadows of an early fall morning from the scattered trees that grew on our side of the basin. We walked forward several yards as quietly as we could over the rough volcanic stones that were hidden beneath the tall grass.

"There they are!" said Burk excitedly as he stretched his arm toward the other slope of the basin.

I don't know what we had expected in this elk paradise, but this was not it. There were, indeed, a dozen black forms among the scattered aspens on the far side of the slope. In an open glade beyond, there were three or four more. But that was all. I am sure that both Bill and I had expected to take our pick from a hundred elk, but we would have to satisfy ourselves with a bare score of the animals.

Most of the basin that formed the crater of San Antonio Mountain was open bunchgrass. Only here and there, fingers of aspen reached down from the volcanic ridges round about to invade the interior crater. These white-trunked trees, with their leafless branches of the fall, offered scant hiding place for any elk herd that might be skulking there. Nonetheless, we swept the entire crater with our glasses to satisfy ourselves that the small herd of elk we had seen at first were the only ones in the whole amphitheater.

"Broomsticks, just broomsticks!" Bill said disgustedly at my elbow. He had been gazing intently with his binoculars at the small group of feeding elk in the aspens.

I focused my glasses on these animals and saw that the herd consisted of about fifteen cows and calves of assorted ages and sizes and two young bulls, apparently still with their mothers. Both bull elk had diminutive antlers, about the size and length of broomsticks, with no indication of tines or prongs on either side. As I unenthusiastically took in these details, there was a muttered curse beside me, a resounding thump and a clatter of small stones.

One of the rounded volcanic pieces that nature had so treacherously put in this place had suddenly rolled from beneath Bill, and he was now struggling on his side, striving to keep his rifle from hitting the hard rock. I saw the elk start in the distance. First, an old cow threw up her head at the clatter of noise that Burk had made. Then, the rest of them stared at us fixedly. In a moment, all the elk swung around and were off together. They galloped through the rough terrain with their typical, ungainly stride and, in a matter of seconds, were over the edge of the crater and into the timber that grew on the slopes beyond.

Elk are animals of fixed habit. They eat at night and bed down during the day, usually picking a patch of thick timber for the latter purpose. Although Burk and I had thought to find the elk on isolated San Antonio Mountain more friendly, we laid our next plans to fit in with the daylight doings of the furtive animals.

"We'll just sweep through those aspen thickets," was the way Burk put it. But sweeping through a few thousand acres of mixed aspen and fir was not as simple as it sounded. We were astonished, however, as we circled the shallow canyons on the farther side of San Antonio Mountain, at the evidence of elk there. The animals had beaten paths that led for a few hundred yards through the thickest stands of timber, then faded away each time as the trails branched and rebranched in a hundred aimless and wandering variations through the forest. Along these elk paths, there was fresh sign in abundance that whole herds of animals had passed that way. Here and there on the aspen trees, we could see where elk antlers had rubbed and massive brow tines had cut away the aspen bark in brown furrows.

The hopes of hunting men run the highest when there is the sure sign of game among the hunting trails. There were elk, some gigantic ones, on San Antonio Mountain, but jumping them from their beds and getting a shot at them was another matter altogether. As we came around the curve of the volcano, we had not seen a single animal, although fresh sign was everywhere.

"These elk have to be somewhere," Burk said for the dozenth time as we looked through vistas of scattered aspen and occasional firs. We stood in an uncertain group in an opening on the shoulder of the mountain. Santiago Yepa touched my shoulder and pointed an outstretched arm. The November wind of late afternoon moved the buckskin fringe on his sleeve. I saw nothing but the vast, open plain that separated San Antonio volcano from the jagged La Plata Mountains in the distance. One peak, with a light-colored, flat face, I knew to be "Broke-Off Mountain," at least ten miles away. Across this grassy distance led a cattle trail with a line of animals moving along it—cattle. Cattle don't have antlers! I snatched my binoculars from the front of my jacket. As they came into focus, there were antlers and the cinnamon circles of elk rumps—hundreds of them. The whole herd was leaving San Antonio Mountain and moving west across open country where elk never go.

"They come back maybe tonight, maybe next night, maybe next spring," Santiago said cheerfully.

The elk herd of San Antonio did not come back to their mountain the next day. We looked. By sundown we had done a complete circuit of San Antonio around the forested slopes of the old volcano and on the crater summit where the pools of water lay innocent of tracks or any sign the elk had drunk there.

"Ghost elk come, then go," Santiago Yepa said, as though summing up a hopeless situation.

As we came down through the elk trails back to our camp late that evening, our requirements for the size of elk horns had diminished considerably. There is a peculiar truism about hunting for horns that short antlers always look longer at the end of the day.

If this was the case at the end of the first day of hunting, it was especially so on the second—and the third—day of our memorable elk hunt. But apparently, some of Santiago's "spirit elk" had "ghosted" back onto San Antonio Mountain, since several times we found small herds of elk in the open glades near the top of the volcano or jumped them from the heavy thickets that grew in the canyons. We even had a glimpse of one head of antlers that might have carried five or six points on a side, but that was all. Again, we thought it strange that elk would cross ten miles of open country. Santiago Yepa thought it only natural that ghost elk appear in one place and then mysteriously appear in another.

"There's only one contemptible mountain," Bill had said a dozen times, "and the elk are here. I've seen a hundred thousand of their tracks. Now where are they?" He glared at me belligerently.

"Maybe they're equipped with radar and walkie-talkies," I suggested in my most amiable manner. "They certainly know where we are, but I'll be damned if I know where they are."

That evening, as we sat around our last campfire, we talked about the elk of San Antonio again, as we had on so many occasions during this exasperating hunt. The night shadows around us and the steely stars of the fall sky seemed to render more plausible Santiago Yepa's stories of this volcanic peak. San Antonio Mountain was a place of spirits.

But, whatever the difficulties might be of this strange place, we had only one last chance. The next morning was the last day of our hunt on San Antonio Mountain. Bill and I had already agreed that any head of horns would be fair game.

The winter constellations were still high in the heavens and there was no hint of eastern light as we breasted the slope of the volcano on that final morning. A spanking wind blew from the north and whipped curls of pumice dust from the bare spots on the ridges around us. We climbed for the most part in silence, as though we feared, by even our whispered comments, to give the ghost elk of San Antonio Mountain a hint of our presence.

Bill Burk and I had decided that we must actually be in the crater amphitheater when the first band of light colored the eastern horizon. These were ghost elk that we were hunting, and, as such, they shunned the daylight, as do all spirits who flourish by night and avoid the full radiance of the sun. So it was that the two of us rounded up over the lip of the crater and felt our way past the small pools of water in its bottom before there was a hint of rosy glow that would mean the morning. In the bottom of this enormous pit, there was a minor lava extrusion, which had been raised there by some auxiliary bubbling and blowing from the molten depths below when the crater was formed. On the previous day, we had marked the spot as a place from which we could see the entire circle of the crater and the water holes at its bottom. We climbed to the top of the small eminence and squatted among some scraggly aspen trees that had sought to find a purchase in the rough lava surfaces. We warmed our numbed hands on our bellies beneath the jackets and waited for the daylight.

The longest minutes on the face of any clock are those just before the dawn. We dared not shift for fear of dislodging some lava stone that would spoil our last opportunity to see the ghost elk of San Antonio. So we waited, just as many hunters have done in a thousand duck blinds or deer stands all over the country, wondering why they had ever come to these cold places where the wind blew so mournfully through the dead limbs of the trees and the light in the eastern sky brightened so slowly.

But at last it did happen—the miracle of the gathering day. At first, we could distinguish trees and rocks a few yards away, then, dimly, the other side of the crater slope and the outline of objects there. Burk plucked at my sleeve.

"Do you see it?" he whispered hoarsely.

"See what?" I asked, although at the same moment, I sensed what he meant.

There was a dark shape, a something that was darker than the darkness before us. The thing couldn't have been more than a hundred yards away, on the grassy slope opposite. It appeared to move, and yet it stayed in the same place. I focused my glasses on the object. At least, it was no stone.

Burk punched me again. "It's an elk! I'm sure it's an elk!" he said excitedly, as he, too, focused his glasses on the spot.

I did not answer, for I was straining with every faculty that I possessed, as though I could, by this concentration, intensify the morning light, which was not strong enough in itself. As we looked at the dark and floating shape, it seemed to stand out more and more from the lighter color of the bunchgrass behind it. It was indeed an elk, and, judging from the outline of the body, it was a massive animal, probably a bull.

We were sure now that the elk was moving, although slowly, and we could make out the head of the animal as he raised and lowered in the slow motion of feeding. I was certain I could see in the glass the dark outlines of branching antlers. Then, as the elk moved a step farther up the hill, some trick of the early morning light glinted upon the polished tines of a dozen points. I saw them all, and I was astounded at the height of the horns above the shoulders of the elk. The graceful curve of the antlers was as high again above the head of the feeding animal as his head was above the ground.

Bill Burke, too, had caught the momentary gleam of polished horn as the feeding elk had raised his antlers high and then stepped forward to take another mouthful of grass on the slope. The bull was moving faster now, as though he sought to gain the protective shelter of the trees on the edge of the crater before any direct ray of sunshine should touch this hallowed spot. The feeding bull was taking two or three steps for every mouthful of grass, and he seemed to chew his forage quickly, as though anxious to be gone.

Burk was already fingering his rifle. I half-raised my own gun, then thought, "Burk won the toss. The first shot today is his." Perhaps I cursed out loud or the evil thought carried against the wind. Suddenly, the monster elk turned broadside to us and looked downward. The breeze still blew toward us, so he could not have our scent, and yet the eyes of his almost black face were almost certainly directed at us where we crouched among the scraggly aspens, like intruders in this sanctified place.

Then the bull turned to go again, trotting nervously up the slope of the crater. In the upper light, we could see more clearly the dark mane on his neck and the palomino color of his battle-scarred flanks. The antlers, too, were plain to the naked eye, and the morning light now showed quite clearly the polished points of the evenly matched tines on either side.

Burk was leveling his gun, then squinting over the barrel, as if he were having trouble finding the elk in his sights. As though sensing this imminent peril, the bull moved more rapidly up the slope, then paused for a fateful moment on the edge of a minor gully washed into the side of the crater by the rains and snows that had fallen here since the lava fires had cooled beneath us.

There, on the edge of the slope, the bull elk looked regal and overpowering in his grandeur. The light exaggerated the massiveness of his body and the tilt of his horns as he laid them back on his withers in preparation for headlong flight. Even as I looked, he gathered his legs beneath him to break into a galloping run that would carry him in a single bound beyond our view.

I opened my mouth to say something. There was a sudden spurt of orange flame beside me, and the blasting crash of Burk's rifle broke the sunrise stillness of that wild place. I was looking at the gigantic bull, and I saw his body swept backward by the impact of the bullet as he disappeared from sight. It was over.

I turned and shook hands with Burk and envied not a little his fortune in bagging one of the gigantic elk of San Antonio Mountain. We walked forward slowly to the spot where the great bull had gone down, and we still talked in a hushed whisper, as though we feared the anger of the spirits that lived here. With not a little anticipation, we topped the small rise where the elk had stood, for we wanted to see just how massive those antlers were.

Together we looked down into the shallow depression of the gully. There was nothing there! Where the body of the big bull should have lain, there were only dead aspen leaves and tufts of withered bunchgrass, innocent of any sign of animal life. Quickly, we looked around us. Above was a scattering of aspen trees, but no place where a massive bull elk could crouch or hide. Beyond was open grassland, too, and yet the elk was gone.

On hands and knees, we searched for telltale drops of blood but found none at all. There was no sign that any such gigantic bull had even been there or that Burk had shot and knocked him kicking on the grass. Bill and I simply stood and looked at each other in amazement.

I can still remember Burk's face as he turned toward me. The morning sun had risen during these exciting moments, and the full light revealed his every feature—the three-day stubble on his chin and the look of wonder in his eyes. "I'll be damned!" was written all over Bill Burk. My own face must have looked the same, for I, too, had seen the elk and had seen him fall. Now there was no sign.

There were a thousand questions that must have bubbled up in our consciousness. Had we ever seen the elk at all, or was it but a trick of the shadows? Perhaps Burk's bullet had hit an antler in the uncertain light and had not really harmed the elk. But, if so, how had the gigantic animal made his escape over the edge of the crater without our seeing him?

There was a sudden rattle of rock behind us. We turned together. A few yards away was another shallow gully. Along the line of this crease in the ground, two enormous sets of tined antlers were moving. Below these racks we saw the dark head with the ears laid back against the skull as the apparition jerked along. The bull elk was sneaking up the gully like a pheasant caught in a ditch.

Burk and I fired together. At the blast of the shots, I saw a spurt of dirt on the edge of the gully where one bullet hit the near side. The dark head of the elk and the massive antlers above disappeared at the sound as though pulled down from below.

"Don't see how he got into that next wash," Bill was saying as we walked forward together.

When we topped the low rise, the depression beyond was as empty as the previous one had been. We stared without comprehension up and down the wash. Nowhere was there a dun-colored body with a pair of matched antlers. The gully was so shallow that it could hardly have hidden the horns of the great bull, much less the bulky body of the animal.

"I've seen quail act like this, but that elk weighs a thousand pounds."

Santiago touched my shoulder. "Ghost elk now there." He pointed behind us.

"But he couldn't . . . ." I stuttered, "he . . . he was . . ."

Below us I saw a movement on the slope. The thing that caught my eye was around the curve of the crater, on the side toward the west, perhaps three hundred yards away. It was a subtle something, all brown and tan, like the grasses and dead leaves that lay thick over the volcanic ground around us. Then it moved again.

"There he is!" I yelled excitedly, "And he's running like the devil."

It was indeed the elk, although somehow he looked different in the distance and carried his antlers tilted so that the beams lay along his back. The bull was running diagonally away from us and breasting the slope with galloping strides that would carry him in a moment to safety over the crater's rim. It was a long shot from a difficult angle, but this was no time to carp about ballistic rules and precedent.

I raised the sight and caught the moving animal in the reticula, then pulled ahead of his nose and fired. Even before my eye left the sight, I saw the brown body of the elk stop in midstride, as though he had tripped on an invisible wire. Then his hind legs flew upward in a gigantic bound, but his front quarters responded not at all. The great animal rolled slowly back down the slope and came to rest against a rock.

Bill Burk and I broke into a run. The spirit elk of San Antonio could not be left unattended for even a few moments. Coming up to the fallen animal, we held our rifles ready and never for a second looked away from the palomino body and the ivory-tipped antlers that moved convulsively in the dry grass. As the dark eyes glazed over in death, Bill went forward and laid his hand on the flank of the animal, as though to assure himself that this, at least, was real.

"Maybe I need to change my glasses," he remarked slowly. "Or perhaps Santiago Yepa was right about the elk on this mountain. Ghost elk are an uncertain cinch."

BIG BEAR OF BELLOTA

CHAPTER XIII

S antiago Chiwiwe was the one who found them. He described them as grandote, and so they were. "Grandote," was a word that Santiago used sparingly and only when he described something that was overpowering and colossal. The other Indians of Jemez Pueblo knew that Santiago never lied and seldom exaggerated. If Santiago said the tracks were "grandote," they were the largest bear tracks in the Jemez Mountains.

If this Jemez Indian, with his usual phlegmatic manner, was all excited about seeing a set of unusual bear tracks, we were even more excited about the prospect of viewing the monster that made the sign. With more than our usual affability, we invited Santiago to get off his sweating horse and ushered the Indian into the ranch house as though he were a chief of his tribe.

Cass Goodner's ranch headquarters is one of those sprawling affairs of logs and frame that radiate hospitality of the old Western variety. The veranda is long and stacked with firewood at one end. A quarter of beef and a bobcat hide hung near the doorway as we eagerly brought Santiago Chiwiwe into the kitchen. Here Vangie Goodner was preparing one of those memorable meals for which she is justly famous. As she lifted the stove lid and poked the burning wood beneath, the red light from the fire danced on the walls and reddened the faces of the people who were gathered in the middle of the room.

There was Cass Goodner himself, with his flat-topped sombrero still pushed back on his head, even there in his own house. Rod Vance, a manager for a large store during his less interesting hours, stood to the side to keep out of Vangie's way as she laid the round table with a red and white checkered cloth. Rod leaned forward to catch any word that Santiago might say about what he had found, but Santiago said nothing at all, as was his way. The Indian squatted on his heels by the woodbox beside the stove and watched with unseeing eyes the preparations for supper in the ranch kitchen.

Rod Vance, Cass Goodner, and I had been hunting bears those past two days. We had ridden hard all over the side of the Jemez that lies above the ranch. It is true that the country behind the San Ysidro was rough in the extreme. The cliffs and canyons of that part of the mountains were dissected and crisscrossed by fault lines that produced a disordered maze of ledges, knife-edge precipices, and protruding rocks.

Over all this geologic jumble in the San Ysidro country, a blanket of vegetation clung precariously. Douglas fir and pine protruded from the rough rocks when their penetrating roots could wring enough moisture from these places. Piñon and juniper colored the lower rocky slopes and minor hills with dull green. In the canyon bottoms, there were occasional clumps of cottonwood that in the fall turned a shimmering flame yellow that rivaled the brilliance of the colored rocks around them. It was an "edgewise country," as Cass called it, usually a bear paradise. Into the rugged breaks and canyons of the San Ysidro, the bears generally came in the fall by the dozens. Of course, it often seemed to us that these hardy animals by nature sought the roughest and rockiest terrain that they could find. Cass had said on more than one occasion, "It all looks level to a bear."

But there was another attraction in the San Ysidro country, even over and above the thousand cliff rincons and hidden gullies, which seemed to make the animals feel secure. On the lower reaches of Semilla Canyon, the red rock gorge funneled out into a series of gently descending flats and terraces. Here some percolating water, flowing beneath the austere ledges of sandstone rock, came to the surface in a number of springs and seeps. Around these dampish spots flourished groves of oak trees growing thickly, with some stems as big around as a man's leg.

These oaks, with their roots deep in the moisture of the springs, fruited every year with graceful hanging clusters of delicious acorns. Even when the oak scrub of the rest of the Jemez was wizened by drought, the benches of Semilla Canyon invariably had mast. Long ago the Spaniards, as they rode their horses beneath these same oaks, had called the spot La Bellota, or "place of the acorns."

The bears of the Jemez country well knew of the Bellota even before Cass Goodner did. Indeed, the location of the bellota groves seemed to be a part of bruin knowledge in these regions even before the Jemez Indians had built their pueblo at the mouth of San Diego Canyon, and that was many centuries ago. Acorns, with bitter tannic acid in their pulp, are difficult food for humans, but to the bear palate, they are pure nectar. This is the stuff that the black bears eat to lay up winter fat when the cool of the fall nights indicated that the time of hibernation was close at hand.

All these things we already knew. On former occasions, the bellota groves had been a sure place to find a bear track. Only the previous season, Cass and I had followed a cherry-colored bear in the same region and had finally treed him in a small x among the rock cliffs. But in the past two days, the gods of the hunt had turned their faces away from us.

The acorns were there and as thick as ever. Every place that we rode, the shells and fruit of the oaks crunched beneath our horses' feet in the game trails. But not a single bear had visited the spot. There were no broken branches where any black bear had pulled down the oaks to get at the mast. There were no tracks and no scuffed sign beneath the trees to show that a bear had passed through the oak groves of the Bellota.

It was for these reasons, especially, that we gathered so eagerly around Santiago Chiwiwe as he sat beside the stove with such a blank look on his face. Rod Vance was just as impatient as the rest of us. We could hardly keep from overwhelming the taciturn Indian with pertinent questions. Santiago had only said, "We find bear tracks, grandote," and he had slid off his horse. That was all.

Cass Goodner was an old hand at these things. The Indians called him White Hat and regarded him as one of themselves. He had learned long ago to be as aggravatingly silent as his pueblo friends. So it was that we talked about cattle prices, about hounds we had known, and about everything else but the subject at hand until supper was over and the dishes had been cleared from the table. There are conventions that must be adhered to in the Southwest. No man is ever questioned on an empty stomach. Also, any news that is good will be even better after an agonizing wait.

"Santiago," Cass began slowly, "you said you found some grandote bear tracks. Where are they?"

Santiago cleared his throat and spat into the woodbox but did not speak for a moment. A light seemed to kindle within his dark eyes, and the wrinkles on his weathered cheeks somehow formed themselves into new lines and creases, as though he saw before him the things of which he spoke.

"Me ride the Senorita—nothing! Then ride the Eureka—nothing!" Here Santiago spread his hands wide as though he had a large armload of nothing at all. "Then circle the Blue Bird Mesa two days. Find there at old mine. Bear sign—big, big." Santiago's cracked fingers formed a circle the size of a dinner plate. "Then saw this track San Miguel rocks." The Indian leaned forward now and paused with the drama of a born orator. "He grandote bear. Come this way. Tracks go San Pablo—now out there."

With a sudden thrust of his arms, he pointed toward the blackened square of the window at the back of the house. The greasy fringe of the sleeve of his hunting jacket swayed with the violence of the motion. In spite of ourselves, we glanced involuntarily toward the same window as though we expected to see the eyes and teeth of a monster bear leering out of the darkness. When we turned back again, Santiago Chiwiwe was calmly readjusting the ribbon that bound up the braids of his hair in a grapefruit-sized bun at the back of his head.

Hunting feeds on hope, and tracks are the stuff of which hope is made. If Santiago Chiwiwe said these tracks were the largest he had ever seen in the Jemez, it was enough.

That night we slept little and then only fitfully. The piñon log in the open fireplace was still a smoldering mound of red embers when we awoke and put on the coffee. It usually took over an hour just to wake up Rod Vance to anything resembling a live human being. On this occasion, however, everyone seemed alert from the very first, and we talked excitedly as we ate in the cold of the ranch kitchen.

"That bear is sure to be in the Bellota," Rod was saying.

"But there isn't a sign of bear in those oaks this year," I reminded him, although not with any particularly pessimistic attitude.

"Santiago said that he trailed him until last night, and he was heading this way. If Santiago said he'll be here, he'll be here," Cass added with finality.

Santiago said nothing but drank his coffee in silence or stirred it slowly with his dirty forefinger. I had noticed before that when there is nothing to be said, Indians keep quiet. It is only we who keep babbling and enthusing when silence is more informative.

Even the horses and the hounds seemed to have been infected with the enthusiasm that Santiago's report had infused in us. The afternoon before, we had dragged back from the hunt with as dispirited a pack of dogs as you ever saw in a city pound. In the briskness of this morning's start, however, our canine trailers bounced around us with barks of enthusiasm. The horses pranced and sidled when we attempted to swing into the cold saddles. The frost crunched beneath their hooves when we started out of the ranch yard. Cass whooped a high-pitched cowboy yell to gather the dogs, and we were off.

There is nothing more thrilling than a morning start with game in the offing. If it were warm on fall mornings, I am sure we would miss much of the thrill of the hunt. The crispness causes one to move quickly, and the spirits soar with the physical exertion.

Far out on the flats of the Ojo del Espirito Santo, there is a volcanic plug of gigantic dimensions. The natives of the place call it the Cabezon, or "Big Head." The sun was just coloring the dark lava of this impressive spire of rock as we crunched through the gravel of the creek at the edge of the San Ysidro Ranch.

We had ridden perhaps a half-mile and had entered the first of the oak groves that are called the Bellota. The light was growing stronger, and we could make out, in the distance, the cliffs and crevices that scar the mouth of Semilla Canyon. With a sudden flapping noise, a hundred band-tailed pigeons swept out of the trees before us and flew noisily away. These wild birds were gorging themselves on the acorns that grew there. But pigeons were small game compared to that which we sought.

Even as the dogs circled wide beneath the trees, we looked in the bare places for possible tracks, but these likely spots were as innocent of sign as before. There were the clean toeprints where a flock of wild turkeys had slowly meandered through this same oak grove to fill their crops with succulent acorns. But of bear tracks, big or little, there was no indication.

The three of us had grown silent after a half-hour of riding, and Santiago Chiwiwe was always that way. As I swung out of my saddle to sweep beneath a particularly low oak limb, I glanced back at the Indian to read from his face some indication of what we might expect. But he gave no sign, not did he speak when he saw me looking at him. He neither smiled nor looked disappointed only rode straight ahead with a certain determination that seemed to radiate confidence. Santiago Chiwiwe knew that we would find the bear.

I swung low again beneath a hanging trunk that had been weighted down by last winter's snow. Branches of unyielding oak twigs struck me full in the face and made a raking noise as I jerked away from the limb. Even after I passed the tree and reached up to catch my hat, the noise continued, as though a thousand angry yellow jackets were imprisoned in one ear.

"It's the dogs!" someone shouted behind me.

I suddenly became aware that our hounds had gone crazy. Every dog that we had was barking and yapping at the top of his lungs. One dark body darted completely beneath my mount, and the horse started violently at the suddenness of the movement. I clamped my knees together to keep my seat in the saddle and looked around bewilderedly. Perhaps yellow jackets? But no, this was fall, and bees of any stinging variety had disappeared with the first frosts.

Both the puppies and the veterans of our pack alternately circled and barked with a bedlam of noise in all directions at once. Even Cass seemed nonplused. We were not chasing anything. It almost seemed as though the dogs were baying at us, which was preposterous for such a well-trained pack of hounds. Even our horses were ill at ease in this strange melee and pranced and fought against the bits.

As suddenly as they had begun, the dogs were still. A single hound stood near the head of my horse with his ears elevated to the alert position and his snout pointing into the wind. Then we heard it, too. It was a crash in the oaks off to one side of the trail. The noise was the swish of a springy young tree as a heavy body brushed against it.

The dogs all looked toward the sound and broke out anew in yaps and shrieks of canine excitement. They were off together like beagles with a rabbit in sight. Only these dogs were not beagles, and none of us thought for a moment that a rabbit could make the crashing and stamping sounds that we heard in the trees.

The oaks in this place dropped off in a gradual slope that descended to the bed of a dry creek. This was a place where a stream flowed only occasionally, when winter's snow melted off the higher ridges in the spring. But on this gently sloping bank, the oak trees grew more thickly than on any other terrace. The hounds slipped easily between the trunks in a scattered, yapping group that was lost in a moment amid the closely growing trees, but to a man on a horse, this oak was murder in a hundred raking, gouging forms.

There is something about the barking of hounds that brings out the worst in humans. I have seen otherwise timid people put their horses at four-foot stone walls simply because a pack of inane dogs up ahead was yapping at a fox. On that insane occasion in the Bellota, our dogs had gone completely crazy, and so did we.

Cass Goodner, leaning low on his horse's neck, leapt past me as though he were taking the water jump at Belmont. His frantic animal, goaded on by the spurs, hit the solid wall of oak trees at the side of the trail with a crash like a collapsing greenhouse. The rest of us spurred our mounts, too, and jumped and hacked through the awful oak in a reckless gallop. A good-sized tree bent beneath my horse's belly as he came down out of a bound, and the poor animal hung there helpless for a few frantic seconds as his hooves churned completely off the ground. Then we crashed on, following the noise and confusion ahead.

Only intermittently, amid the noise of splintering oak branches and the thrashing of dead leaves against my hat, could I hear anything at all. When I could, it was the voices of hounds only a few yards beyond. The dogs were growling and baying, and some of their voices sounded muffled, as though they barked with their mouths full of meat.

My horse saw it first, for I was bending low, half out of the saddle and with my hat knocked over my eyes. This gelding that I rode was a stout and even-tempered animal that, to my certain knowledge, had packed many a deer and not a few bear out of the same rough country. In the presence of fresh blood or ordinary excitement, this horse never twitched an ear or so much as whinnied in fright. But, as we cleared the last oaks, the docile animal suddenly shied as skittishly as a carriage mare at a thunderclap.

I was thrown violently to the side and ignominiously drooped from the saddle like a broken shoestring in a footrace. Another bound of the horse shook me clear, and I dropped and rolled over on the very edge of the wash. My mouth and hands were full of gravel as I got up to look for my treacherous horse. Instead, I saw the head and forequarters of a gigantic bear.

My horse, with my rifle in the saddle boot, galloped off down the wash with a pounding of frantic hooves. In the second that followed, the bear did not look at me as I sprawled on the ground. Still hampered by my chaps, I rolled clear of the milling dogs that danced and circled over my prone body as though I were an integral part of the scenery underfoot.

At first, I could see only the bear's head and neck, because his lower portions were obscured by the advancing and retreating hounds in front of him. Then, all at once, the beleaguered animal rose on his hind legs to fight the dogs from that height. I was on my knees, attempting to rid myself of my chaps so that I could move my legs, but instead I stared, openmouthed, at the towering beast beyond. It was a giant bear. I could almost hear Santiago Chiwiwe saying, over the tumult of the barking, "See, I tell you this bear is grandote."

The head of the animal looked as big as a bushel basket, but I had little opportunity to make comparisons, for the bear laid back his lips and lunged at a dog that came too close. The bear's head looked almost round, his ears pressed back against his skull. Even his nose seemed out of place, turning straight up on the end of his snout to lay bare a solid row of gleaming teeth.

Standing straddle-legged on his hind legs, the furious animal plied his paws from both sides. The curved claws that stuck beyond his toes looked as long as the tines of a pitchfork and certainly would be as deadly if any of them caught the underbelly of an unwary hound. Time and again, the gigantic bear fell forward as some dog came close and sought to gather the audacious hound between those frightful jaws. Each time, as the light-footed dogs bounced warily out of his reach, the bear closed his teeth with a noise like the slamming of a steel gate. He ground his teeth together and saliva flew in bloody strings from his mouth as he turned his head from side to side to meet each new onslaught.

During the noise and confusion, the other men had dismounted and somehow gotten their horses out of the battle area. Cass was yelling something over the tumult that sounded like, "Save the dogs!" although I couldn't see at the moment what we could do about it. Rod Vance came in from the side with his rifle in his hand. I saw him raise the weapon once, then lower it reluctantly as the dogs surged quickly about their antagonist in a melee of moving tails and teeth.

The bear, in the middle of the hound pack, suddenly bellowed like a range bull in a fight and charged the dogs and us as well. It was plain to see that this bear was far too heavy to climb a tree, even if there had been a sizable one close at hand. The fur that rippled on his flanks and shoulders told of layered fat beneath that skin, built up these last few weeks by tons of acorns that the animal had consumed. So ponderous was the huge animal that he could not even run to find some refuge in the cliffs and ledges so close above us.

He was a black bear, it is true, but in color not all black, for his coat had a brownish sheen as he turned and twisted in the morning sun. The hair seemed dark at the base and the color of antique mahogany on the tips. The cold Jemez nights had thickened the fur on his pelt until it was as fine and silken as that of a Northern fox.

All these things were noted, like the backdrop of a play. They were there but not the focal points of attention. None of us could keep his eyes from the flashing teeth and swinging claws of the animal as he rose or fell forward to attack the dogs. Never once did the bear so much as glance in our direction or indicate by any look from his little red-rimmed eyes that he even knew we were there. It was a death battle that we witnessed. The only question was how many deaths there would be.

Cass was bawling again above the tumult, "Quick, shoot, close in!" To add emphasis to his words, he grabbed Vance's arm and jerked him toward the bear as though he wanted to offer his friend as a sacrifice under the sledgehammer paws of this monstrous animal. Then I saw it. It was Pancho, the Airedale. This remarkable dog was supposed to be a house pet, but he had been on so many hunts with Cass that he undoubtedly considered himself the mainstay of the bear pack.

Pancho was a peculiar duality. He could be as gentle as a newborn kitten or a raging storm of flashing white teeth and hideous growls. It was Pancho, now, with this Airedale temper that precipitated the end. The dog somehow worked his way behind the antagonists and in one sudden leap jumped clear onto the bear's back and seized the animal by the side of the face. In the swirl and surge of the fighting, Pancho was an added lump of furiously clawing fur and feet on the very top of the bear's head.

The astounded bear ducked ludicrously as though a bee had stung him unexpectedly in an unprotected place. He raised both paws to his face and brushed furiously at the dog on his head. It would have been funny had we not known that Pancho's death was only inches away. For a second, the audacious dog clung to one bear ear, chewing that unprotected organ unmercifully and clawing the side of the bear's face. Then one huge paw swung from behind. The hooked claws in unison caught behind Pancho's shoulders and swept him forward as inevitably as doom itself.

For an awful second, the bear held the Airedale between his paws like a squirrel about to crack a nut; then the huge head bent forward and those frightful jaws opened like the white-rimmed mouth of hell. There was a sickening crunching of fiber and flesh, and Pancho dropped limply at the bear's feet. At the same moment, a deafening blast of noise blotted out all other sounds.

Rod Vance was among the dogs with a smoking rifle in his hand. Quickly, he levered another shell into the gun and fired again point blank into the bear's neck. A puff of fur flew out behind as the bullet carried through. The brown bear looked up, surprised at this interruption. His little bear eyes seemed to focus for the first time on the forms of men.

The eyes of the bear seemed suddenly darker as he stood there with his paws hanging useless in midair. Those eyes misted over like a hazy cloud drifting before the sun. The great body stood a moment more there among the dogs, reluctant to give way. Then, without a sound, the huge animal slumped forward and sagged in a heap of formless fur on the ground. A great muscle twitched somewhere beneath the brown fur on the shoulder of the beast, and he was still. A trickle of blood from between his open jaws rolled out onto the dirt of the ground.

Everyone else seemed stunned by the abruptness of the end. Only Cass leapt forward to seize one of the gigantic paws and roll the carcass away from the Airedale. Pancho lay as lifeless as the bear, and we carried him gently out and laid him on the oak leaves. As Cass put his hand behind the foreleg of the fearless animal, we held our breath. He nodded slowly. Pancho's heart was still beating. In a few moments, the jaws of the Airedale trembled a little and a red tongue licked out over his bruised lips. His eyes flickered open, and he seemed to recognize friends, for he licked our hands when we held him.

Even today, Pancho has a patch of light-colored skin on the side of his head where the teeth of the big bear had torn the flesh away from his skull. This Airedale is one of those few pioneer spirits to be scalped and live to tell about it.

We turned to Santiago Chiwiwe. From somewhere out of his tattered clothing, he had resurrected some red and yellow paint. Across his cheeks and the bridge of his nose, he had smeared a broad band of vermilion. Bears are animals of potent medicine in Jemez Pueblo, and the giant bear of Bellota was a great spirit, indeed.

"Grandote—sure big grandote," Santiago mumbled to himself as he gingerly swung back one of the limp paws of the great animal. "Lots of meat, lots of trouble. We get both."

WHITE GHOST BEAR

CHAPTER XIV

His eyes were the color of fresh blood on a handful of snow as he stalked along the edge of the village. It was the pink iridescence of the eyes that the terrified inhabitants saw first and the white coat of the bear afterwards. The fur of the magnificent animal was as white as a moonbeam but somehow unwholesome in its whiteness—and certainly unnatural on a bear. Obviously, the thing was a demon, with sullen eyes that looked out through some covering of white that he donned as a disguise. The people of Jemez Pueblo shrank back from their doorways and covered their faces from the apparition.

The Indians of the Jemez tribe are no different from other pueblos of New Mexico in their respect for bears. Anyone will tell you that these animals are powerful medicine and redolent with spiritual essence that radiates from their bodies. A Jemez Indian who dares to kill a bear is a brave man among many courageous men, but such an audacious pueblo hunter had better have his own spiritual medicine in order!

Even to touch an ordinary bear requires the contaminated person to spend the subsequent five days in the ceremonial kiva enacting purification ceremonies and to culminate these rituals with a feast for the whole village. Indeed, so great is the power of bears that many a stout Jemez hunter will not disturb one of the animals under any circumstances or even step in a bear track.

If an ordinary black bear had come down from the Jemez Mountains and stalked through Jemez Pueblo, it would have been an awesome indication. But a white bear!

It had been broad afternoon when the spirit bear showed himself along the river bank in Jemez town. That same night, the long-haired old men gathered in the kivas in consternation. So terrifying a sign had not appeared in the Rio Grande Valley since the Spaniards had come, bringing the Christian cross with them. Old chieftains, with faces wrinkled by the southwestern suns of eighty seasons, told of all the experiences they knew that might suggest what spirit it was and why he appeared in white skin.

When morning came over the eastern cliffs of San Diego Canyon, the smoke from the council fires still curled out of the hatchways of the kiva roofs. The drone of the old men's voices showed that the meaning of the visitation of the white bear had not yet been discovered. But ordinary men could see by the morning light that a streak of white lay through the plaza where the phantom animal had passed. It was as though the Milky Way had fallen and left its mark across the ground from the hills to the east of the pueblo extending to the creek on the far side where the bear had disappeared. Of course, some matter-of-fact souls said that the white mark was only gypsum washed there during the recent rains, but these doubters were not those who had actually seen the moonbeam bear pass that way.

As the chiefs still wrangled in the kivas, the curse of whiteness fell upon Jemez Pueblo. A mist rose from the river and drifted over the town. The mountains behind were blotted out by the whiteness. Even trees and adobe house terraces close at hand floated in vapor that had no perspective and lacked reality. Most of the Indians had never before seen fog, which is usually unknown in the arid realms of the Southwest.

That whole day, the white mists clung in San Diego Canyon. Wisps of cotton cloud covered the red cliffs. Even the rooftops where the people gathered to look at the phenomenon were not visible from the plazas, nor one house tier from another. Cloying dampness glistened on the viga poles and even on the clothing of the inhabitants as they stood dumbly in the midst of the whiteness.

On the next day, the old men, who had fasted during the crisis, gathered together the two halves of the populace, the Turquoise and the Squash people, in the dancing plaza. The chief of the Badger Clan, who knows all things, spoke solemnly. "The white bear is an evil spirit which has come among us. His whiteness will fade the green from the growing corn and the red from living blood." He looked around the crowd of silent Indians as he spoke. The faces of the townspeople seemed already ashen in the unholy light, as though the white curse was even then at work in their veins.

"The spirit bear must be killed," the chief continued, "by one of you." The front rows of the closely packed people shrank back from the speaker. There was none among them who wanted to be pointed out to hunt the white bear. "The killing must be done with the sacred bow and arrow of the hunting ceremony and not with a gun. When the arrows strike the white bear, the mountains will tremble."

None doubted the chief's words, and none was so curious as to test them by volunteering for the hunt.

The speaker added, with obvious knowledge of the ways of men, "He who kills the white bear dares the power of evil medicine but gains a great medicine in return. The skin which the spirit wears as a covering will make this man the most powerful of all men."

There was silence in the dance plaza as the people stared stolidly before them and thought upon the words of the Badger Chief. Slowly Sidro Sebaquiu stepped forward. The chief handed him the bow and arrow quiver, then pointed to the west where the bear had gone. Sidro Sebaquiu started off into the mists with the certain feeling that every eye was upon him as he walked away.

Sidro was then in his twentieth year. This is the tender age when young men have lived long enough to find out that they know everything and not long enough to discover that their knowledge is only a single grain of sand in the desert of life. Sidro Sebaquiu wore his hair long in the conservative manner, with a red ribbon catching up the braids in a bun at the back of his head. He flaunted a blue shirt from the store and leather leggings he had made himself, with high moccasins to match. His usually impassive face, with high arching nose, was thrust forward in a determined manner. The murmur of admiration that came faintly to his ears from the people in the plaza had caused him to square his shoulders and stride forward swiftly toward the mountains.

There is a courage in all of us that is strong before the eyes of others but ebbs away when we are alone. As Sidro passed the last tier of adobe houses that marked the limits of the Jemez village, the drifting fog closed around him like the menacing fingers of spirit hands. He was afraid and regretted deeply the brashness that had caused him to step out before the others and take the sacred bow and arrows from the hands of the Badger Chief.

Sidro stopped in his indecision. The sacred bear was not to be taken by a white man's gun, the chief had said. Sidro Sebaquiu had such a gun, and it killed at a distance with the power of thunder.

With the thought, Sidro turned and skirted the dim corrals and piles of fodder that marked the edges of the town. By this route, he could avoid the eyes of any of the townspeople that were still gathered in the plaza. With a furtive manner, he approached his own pueblo room from the rear. Silently, he slipped in, unobserved, as he hoped, by any of his friends.

From its place under the roof beams, he pulled out an ancient rifle, a Winchester of archaic vintage and weathered appearance. Sidro swept his fingers along the barrel to clear away the dirt and cobwebs. He worked the lever tentatively, and the rusty metal screeched with the unaccustomed movement. From a niche in the wall, he took three brass cartridges that fitted the gun and carefully fed them into the magazine.

With these preparations, Sidro the hunter felt more at ease, although he glanced cautiously around before he once again stepped out behind the pueblo and circled the corrals away from the village. He slung the forbidden rifle over one shoulder by a leather thong that ran from muzzle to stock. The gun had been in the dirt of the pueblo roof so many years it probably wouldn't fire anyway, but it was good to feel its metal weight tugging at his shoulder as he walked.

Beyond the willows of the river, the mists that had enclosed Jemez Pueblo so mysteriously seemed lighter, and in places the air was clear for a few yards, with white veils of vapor only along the tops of the trees. On the bank, Sidro found the tracks of the bear. The animal had walked through the water, as all bears do, and tramped up and down a mud bar on the far side. From a welter of imprints, a straight set of bear tracks led away toward the west. The outlines of the animal's feet were of no tremendous size but were somehow ominous in their clarity in the moist mud of the Jemez River. As Sidro followed them with his eye, pale vapor radiated up from the imprints like smoke from a smothered fire. It had been many hours since the bear had passed that way, and yet the spirit medicine still rose from the trail where the beast had walked.

The ghost bear had not stepped lightly. A child could have followed the animal, for the imprints of the feet were plainly marked, even on the hard ground. But no child, nor even an ordinary man, would have kept on that trail. Sidro Sebaquiu was as brave as most, but even he thought more than once of turning back and mingling in the security of his friends as they waited in the plaza.

Two thoughts drove him on as he mounted the first of the timbered ridges on the far side of the valley. He felt shame at the contemplation of appearing so soon before the townspeople and telling them that his will had been too weak to follow the white bear. Also in Sidro's thoughts, as he breasted the slopes, was the burning desire to be the possessor of the white bearskin. That would be a trophy more powerful than any other medicine in Jemez.

By this combination of circumstances, Sidro Sebaquiu was forced to continue along the plain trail of the moonbeam bear. He kept well to one side of the tracks and avoided even stepping over them as he traced their course up a side canyon and thence along the comb of a raking ridge that led toward the high lava cliffs above. The white bear, just as ordinary animals of his kind, evidently knew the country well, for the trail led surely up those ridges and spurs where gaps in the barrier cliffs appeared like magic out of the mists.

Even the drifting layers of white fog thinned as Sidro climbed higher. Once or twice, the world cleared before him and he could see the green-clad bulk of Rodondo Mountain far in the distance. Below, in San Diego Canyon, Jemez Pueblo remained hidden by the smoky stuff that filled the gorge like milky water in a deep lake. Occasionally, too, Sidro thrilled to the spirit of the hunt and almost forgot that the quarry was a bear with fur as white as milkweed down. Late in the day, he found where the animal had eaten on a dead deer and then lain down beneath the limbs of a close-growing spruce. From among the needles of the lower limbs of the tree, Sidro picked, with a reverent hand, a little tuft of white hair. He could feel the tingle of the medicine in the thing as he carefully placed the hairs in a pouch at his belt.

That night, Sidro Sebaquiu, the famous hunter, slept with his eyes open. The wet woods about him were full of the murmur of living things, although there was no wind. Owls talked back and forth to each other. The cry of an owl means death is coming. Far up on the mountain, a cat screamed as though to tell the world that strange things moved in the Jemez night—and nothing slept.

A watchful night is no hardship for an Indian hunter, but Sidro was hollow-eyed in the morning. It was not the sleeplessness that made his muscles weak and his back feel weary. It was the tense hope that he would see before him the round contours of a ghost white bear and yet the dread of the sight when it should come.

On that next morning, much of the mist had cleared from the

higher mountain, but the trees still dripped moisture from their needles and the air felt wet in the hunter's throat. As Sidro moved out through the damp woods of the upper ridges, he had difficulty following the bear tracks at all. In places where the animal had walked on pine needles and across the forest duff, the resilient stuff showed little indication that a heavy body had passed that way. Even with these difficulties, however, Sidro did not lose his hunt instincts. He loosened the string on the sacred bow that he carried, for the moisture had tightened the twisted rawhide almost to the breaking point. The arrows, too, he tested with his eye, then straightened the warped shafts between his teeth. He felt, with the sure knowledge of a born hunter, that the quarry was near.

Even the sodden sticks underfoot he avoided with his moccasined feet so that no soft snap or shuffle would betray his presence. With scrupulous care, he avoided downhanging branches, drooping with the weight of the droplets of moisture that made them heavy. As he moved through the trees, he twisted his shoulders first to one side, then to the other, so that no dead aspen twig or clutching tuft of pine would touch his person or brush against the rifle that he carried on his back. Sidro the hunter was stalking his prey.

The predatory animal senses the nearness of game with sensitive nostrils. It may be that Sidro Sebaquiu had tracked in the Jemez woods for so many years that he, too, could smell the hot body odor of the larger animals. Whether it was scent or sense, however, it is certain that the Indian grew more alert as he walked among the wet trees at the very top of the Jemez ridges.

On the mountain above San Diego Canyon, the spines of the finger ridges come together like the palm of a hand. In this place, on the very crest of the range, is a series of volcanic cliffs that form a rough circle with a plateau above them. This elevation rises from the irregular slopes around like a massive medieval tower standing alone above a ruined town. The structure was formed many geologic ages ago when the Jemez Mountains were smelted by volcanic fires and torn by earthquake rumblings that elevated these same cliffs and tumbled the great rock fragments from their faces to form a ragged screen below.

The dim trail of the white ghost bear led Sidro straight toward the citadel cliffs and the rock piles that lay beneath them. Along the talus slope below the lava walls, the trees thinned out and there were spaces of bare ground. Even here, however, the tracking was difficult, and Sidro paced back and forth with his head bent forward close to the ground so that his dark eyes might detect any slight depression or the disturbed position of a single twig.

Suddenly, from around the curve of the volcanic rock ahead, a jay squawked. It was the cry of an angry bird that scolds an intruder in its domain. Sidro stiffened and straightened up. There were scattered trees and clumps of occasional bushes among the rocks at the foot of the cliffs. Through these he could see nothing. But around the shoulder of the dark stone above the verdure, a white finger of mist drifted out as though pulled by an invisible force in the still air. There was a muffled thud of a muddy rock close by, as a heavy foot turned it from its socket in the talus.

Again, Sidro Sebaquiu crouched low and moved forward. As he did so, he unslung the bow from its cover and automatically tested the string with his thumb. If the spirit bear was moving at the base of the cliffs, he would be behind that next clump of mountain mahogany. As Sidro pulled even with the screening bushes, he shifted the quiver of arrows higher onto his shoulder and reached back for a feathered shaft.

With the suddenness of unexpected death, the brush crashed apart before him. The red-mouthed head of destruction itself broke through the leaves. There were a black nose, slavering teeth, and white ears laid back in anger against the animal's head. Through the two red holes on either side of the muzzle, the demon within the white skin looked straight at the Jemez Indian with eyes that burned like live coals fanned by the wind.

Sidro Sebaquiu, hunter and tracker though he was, remained frozen where his last step had taken him. He still had one arm poised over his shoulder reaching for the arrow that his fingers never found. His mouth had dropped open as the ghost bear charged through the branches, but the Indian neither moved nor cried out.

Time stood still, there on Jemez Mountain. The hunter did not draw his arrow, and the white bear did not lunge forward but remained half-erect through the middle of the bush, with his mouth open and his red eyes burning hate.

But time will not remain long stationary, nor will fate stop its inexorable course to wait on any man. Perhaps it was the low growl that rumbled from between the teeth of the white bear. It may have been that the muscles of Sidro Sebaquiu had been tensed too long and his hunter's mind had conjured up just such an awful vision as now stood before him. The sacred bow of the Jemez people dropped from his nerveless fingers and rolled sideways onto the wet leaves.

As though this were a signal, Sidro retreated a step, then another, while his eyes stared fascinated at the form of the bear before him. It is to his everlasting credit that he did not turn and bolt. The stern fiber of a long line of hunters stiffened his resolve, even as he retreated again before the awful eyes of the moonbeam bear. His nerveless hands dropped to his sides. His palm twitched with cold sweat, and the steel buttplate of the gun on his back felt cold against his wrist.

The gun! With a nervous hitch of his shoulders, Sidro slipped the thong and brought the rusty rifle around under his arm. Jerkily, he pumped the dilapidated mechanism. Even with dirt and the dripping moisture of the wet forest saturated through the complaining parts, the slide flipped the shell into place and the breach closed home.

At the mechanical noise made by the iron, the bear raised his snout a trifle higher, then rose with a heave to his hind legs. Sidro could see in one awful moment that the claws of the animal's forepaws were black against his white belly. The unnatural fur of the beast was yellowed in places, and matted, but these details were only the framing for the fascination of the face of the spirit bear. It was the eyes and the teeth that radiated the omnipresence of evil medicine.

Mechanically, Sidro Sebaquiu raised the rifle. Even though his eyes did not squint down the sights, he jerked viciously at the trigger of the weapon. The blast of the shot was deafening against the cliffs, and the corner of the rifle stock dug a bloody furrow in Sidro's shoulder. A spurt of fur flew from the belly of the bear, and a look of surprise seemed to pass over those animal features. Feverishly, Sidro levered another shell into the Winchester. Again he jerked on the trigger as he held the weapon half-cradled in his arms. The recoil of the second shot carried the rifle completely out of his hands, but again, there was a movement of fur on the breast of the bear, as though a tiny draft of wind had parted the hair for an instant.

Sidro did not look down to where the rifle had skidded against the bole of a small tree. He had performed these acts mechanically, like a man in a nightmare who grasps at any weapon to fend off an apparition. Even after the second shot, the red eyes of the spirit bear seemed to burn through his own. Sidro thought for one terrible instant that spirit bears were invulnerable to any weapon. He was doomed.

Again there was a rumbling growl from the bear's open mouth. A drop of crimson blood welled up from between the white teeth and stained the fur at the animal's throat. Then a welter of red drops followed the first and the growl gurgled to a whisper like a dying wind. A tremor seemed to shake the white body, beginning at the ends of the paws. Without another sound, the great body pitched forward and fell with a sodden thump almost at the Indian's feet.

The people of Jemez say that the white mists cleared from the pueblo at the very instant when the bear was killed. Nor has there been a fog in these dry mountains since the time that the spirit in white bear's clothing visited San Diego Canyon.

But the tribe did not come completely unscathed through these terrible events. Sidro Sebaquiu, himself, became afflicted with the whiteness. His skin turned pale and his hair became like straw. The color faded from his eyes and the blood showed through with the raw redness that had marked the eyes of the ghost bear.

The spirit whiteness touched some of Sidro's relatives as well, so they also lost their coloring, and their eyes became reddish-pink under the influence of the bear medicine. It is true that in the kiva there hangs, even now, a bearskin with fur the color of a moonbeam. It is small wonder, with this powerful talisman in their possession, that these Indians flourish and are one of the most powerful and important tribes among all the pueblos. But any Jemez hunter will tell you that a white ghost bear should be killed only with an arrow.

KIMO AND THE ANTELOPE

CHAPTER XV

T he mass of jostling brown bodies and flashing hooves rumbled through the jaws of the trap. Kimo, crouching behind the wall of brush on one wing, counted twenty-times-twenty antelope and perhaps more. The other Indians, bending low behind the lines of brush that formed the V-shaped trap, fingered their bows and placed iron-tipped arrows on their bowstrings. The six war captains at the point of the long brush enclosure raised their repeating Winchesters and sighted along the barrels. At the narrow end of the trap, the antelope herd would pass between the walls of branches and sticks no wider apart than a village street. There the kill would be the greatest. All the hunters, some forty men, had taken off their bright-colored headbands so as not to frighten the antelope. All had painted their faces with dark red ocher. Red is the color of blood and meat.

At the wide mouth of the trap, the long lines of brush and fallen trees were a long arrow shot apart. Once the antelope had galloped through this opening, ten men under Kimo's direction would move forward, each man carrying a section of bristling juniper brush in front of him. With these brush sections, they would close the mouth of the trap behind the antelope here. Every animal inside would be within arrow range.

When the Indian hunters, instructed by Kimo, had first stampeded the antelope from the benches above the Plains of St. Augustine, the animals had run uncertainly. The bucks, especially one large buck with wide-spreading black horns, ran last. He had looked at the Indian hunters contemptuously. This one antelope seemed to know the killing range of a bow and arrow, and even of a .44-40 Winchester. Howling like wolves and waving blankets, the Indians had turned the milling antelope in the direction of the brush trap built among the piñon trees above the plain. Here, there was a place between two low hills where the antelope often moved on their way to water. The scattered piñon trees made good cover. Finally, the circling herd had strung out at a dead run toward the trap. As the howling human hunters moved in close, waving their blankets, the big-horned Chief Antelope moved swiftly from the rear to the front. Faster than any horse could gallop, the whole herd bunched and ran directly between the wings of the trap.

Kimo was breathless but exultant as he held up his hand to signal the men with the sections of brush to close in behind the antelope herd. Already the Chief Antelope was well between the brush walls. On both sides, the hunters tensed. In a moment, the milling herd would be trapped. Each hunter would rise from his hiding place. Every arrow would find a mark.

Kimo dropped his arm. At that instant, the Chief Antelope slid to a stop. The whole herd behind him stopped abruptly, as though jerked back by some unseen hand. The Chief Antelope had seen something or smelled something. He wheeled. Racing at full speed again, he dashed back through his own herd. Kimo could see the widespread black horns of the big Chief Antelope cutting through the other animals. The rest of the antelope turned. In a torrent, they poured back again through their own dust. Before anyone could loose a single arrow, the whole herd was out of the trap and running back toward the open plain.

The men with the brush sections dropped their loads. Most of the hunters behind the brush walls stood up to watch as the antelope escaped. It was done. The Bear God had warned the Chief Antelope. Some of the hunters raised their bows and looked menacingly at Kimo.

The escape of the antelope herd on the Plains of St. Augustine was not the first disaster that had befallen Isleta Pueblo on the Rio Grande of New Mexico. All of the bad fortune had begun two years ago. It was Kimo who started it.

Kimo, which means "mountain lion" in the language of the Pueblo Indians of the Rio Grande, had been born under a lucky star. As a boy, he had seen the vision of a mountain lion and so had been given the name of that powerful hunting animal. When Kimo was less than twenty winters old, he became chief of the Caiyaik, the hunting society of Isleta Pueblo. Because the mountain lion is considered the most powerful hunter of all, it was logical that Kimo should be chief, even though he was very young.

Kimo led the Caiyaik Society on many successful hunts. He and other hunters made two long trips into the flatlands far east of their native Rio Grande Valley. Here, they hunted with Jicarilla Apaches and Kiowas for the buffalo of the plains along the Red River. They brought back much dried buffalo meat and many buffalo robes to the pueblo. This meat helped greatly to keep Isleta Pueblo flourishing when the pueblos were having difficulty with crop failures because of drought and with the American government. White settlers were encroaching on their land. The U.S. Army was trying to keep each Indian group on a reservation. There was much trouble. Then, in 1884, the last of the buffalo herds disappeared.

Through these trying times, Kimo was able to help the Isleta people find a new life. The Pueblo Indians are essentially farmers, but Kimo was a hunter, and he and the young men of the Caiyaik Society were able to supplement their scanty food supply by now bringing in many deer from the mountains. Kimo was ever careful to observe all the rituals of his forefathers so that the spirit of the deer would never be offended. The faces of the hunters were always painted red. Pieces of the killed deer were always set aside as food for the Beast Gods. The eyes of the deer were always taken back to the mountains so that these eyes would grow another deer ready for the bows and arrows of the hunting society the next year.

Kimo had brought back from his hunts on the plains two ideas to help the food supply of the Isleta tribe. One of these was a new kind of bow, which Kimo had found the Kiowas using to hunt buffalo. Such a bow was double-curved and bound with sinew from the back of a buffalo or an elk. A sinew-backed bow could drive an arrow twice as far and much more powerfully than an ordinary wooden bow. Although the American soldiers kept the Indians from buying guns, the war chiefs of Isleta had managed to get some of the new Winchesters that fired many shots. Kimo himself preferred a Kiowa bow and arrows tipped with iron cut from the metal tire of a wagon wheel. A well-made arrow, shot from a sinew-backed bow, was lethal and silent.

From the Plains hunters, Kimo had also picked up ways of hunting antelope that were always successful. Approaching near a feeding herd, Kimo would creep close until the antelope raised their heads to look. Then he lay on his back in the grass and kicked his feet in the air. The naturally curious antelope were never able to resist coming close to see what the two moving objects might mean. Kimo then jumped erect and shot the nearest animal with his bow.

The Isleta women had plenty of deer and antelope skins to tan and whiten into boots when Kimo led the Caiyaik Society. Everyone in the pueblo had plenty of dried meat. The war captains mumbled, of course, that the American soldiers would not let them fight, as in olden times. The war captains found some excitement by joining Kimo and his Caiyaiks on many hunts. The hunting of deer and the antelope was almost as much fun as war, so everyone was content—that is, until that one day in the early winter, three seasons after the buffalo disappeared. On that day, Kimo went hunting by himself in the Manzano Mountains, on the east edge of the Rio Grande Valley.

Kimo had observed all the rituals so that the Chief of the Deer would let one of his tribe be killed. Kimo was tracking a large buck in the snow. Just ahead of him, the oak brush shook so that dried leaves fell off in the snow. He saw the curve of the deer's back through the moving bush. Above the bush, antlers moved back and forth as though the buck was polishing his horns. Kimo drew back his sinew-backed bow until the arrowhead touched his hand. He let it go. The arrow tore through the moving oak brush. Kimo heard the solid thud as the arrow sank home in flesh. He ran forward. There on the red-splotched snow was not a deer but a brownish-colored bear! The feathered end of the arrow stood out in the bear's throat. The animal thrashed and rolled on the snow with blood flying from his open jaws. He tried to bite the arrow, but it was too close below his mouth, in his neck.

Kimo ran the whole fifteen miles back to the pueblo. He did not stop to see if the bear was dead. All the Pueblo Indians are afraid of the powerful medicine carried in the body of a bear. At Isleta Pueblo, the bear is the most powerful of the Beast Gods, even more so than the mountain lion. No Isleta hunter will even step in a bear's tracks for fear of bear magic.

All the Indians of Isleta Pueblo gathered around Kimo when they heard of the disaster. Which was the stronger medicine—the hunting power of the mountain lion or the magic of the bear, chief of all the Beast Gods? The town chief of Isleta, Pablo Abeyta, declared that the whole pueblo was in such danger that they could take no chance on the outcome. Pablo Abeyta called together the Medicine Society in the kiva. There, the Medicine Society members organized a great cure, just as they would for any other great sickness. Kimo was directed to stay in his house for four days, alone, without seeing his wife or his family. At the end of the fourth day, all the members of the Medicine Society came into his house and spat upon Kimo to drive out the spirit of the bear. They rubbed the sacred eagle feathers before his eyes. Finally, Pablo Abeyta pronounced the words, "The bear is still alive. He will come to you. You have left half of your heart in the mountains."

At these words, a member of the Medicine Society, dressed in a bearskin, appeared at the edge of the village. All the people cowered in their houses and hid their eyes. The bear came straight to Kimo's house and pounded on the door with his paw. He entered, carrying a bowl of a white drink that contained a most powerful medicine concocted by the Medicine Society. As Kimo drank the bitter white drink, he drank back the other half of his heart. The Medicine Man, dressed as a bear, went back to the kiva and took off his costume. The town and Kimo were saved from the black magic of the Beast Gods.

But it did not turn out that way. The evil of the bear was still in the village, and it still sat on Kimo's shoulder. The very next month, the Caiyaik Society held the annual rabbit hunt in the Rio Grande Valley below Isleta. As Kimo called the Caiyaik Society together to organize the hunt, it began to snow. In spite of all this, Kimo enacted all the ancient ceremonies to call the rabbits together and to appease the Rabbit Chief for taking some of his people. The members of the Caiyaik Society armed themselves with their sickle-shaped rabbit clubs. They formed a great circle in the brushlands along the river. Shouting to the Rabbit Chief to bring his people, all the hunters came together in a circle. Behind them, other townspeople waited with clubs to kill any rabbits that might break through the inner line. The hunters drew together into a smaller and smaller circle. Cottontails and jackrabbits were flashing between the thick-growing bushes. As the hunters held their clubs high to make the first casts, the rabbits seemed to disappear. The circle closed in. The last rabbit was gone. The old men of the pueblo could never remember a rabbit hunt at which not a single rabbit was killed.

On the way back from the rabbit hunt, the people were silent and moved away from Kimo and the bad medicine of the bear that sat on his shoulder. But it was not only Kimo who had incurred the anger of the Bear Chief. It was the whole town. That winter, not a single member of the Caiyaik Society brought in a deer. Pablo Abeyta and his Medicine Society put on a special ceremony to call down the deer from the mountains. Not a single animal fell to their bows or guns.

Hunting and the hunting society normally furnishes meat for ceremonial purposes and to supplement the corn, beans, and squash of the normal pueblo diet. But the next summer, after Kimo had killed the brown bear, the corn cropped failed. There was no rain, and the Rio Grande shrank to a mere rivulet in its sandy bed. The Dark Eyes Society put on three special rainmaking ceremonies, but there was no rain.

By the next winter, the pueblo was in a desperate situation. During the late summer and fall months, Kimo had led his Caiyaiks on several antelope hunts to the west of the valley. They killed not a single antelope at this time, although they tried every stratagem that they knew. One particular buck antelope, with very widespread horns, seemed to be the one that always alarmed the others, so that they ran out of bowshot. This Chief Antelope had gathered most of the other animals together in a large herd that normally fed in the middle of the great plain called St. Augustine. In this place, it was impossible for any hunter to get close enough to make a kill.

Kimo watched the antelope for a great many days. He planned to make a trap of brush and trees on the edge of the plain. This trap would be shaped like the ripples in the water when a beaver swims through a quiet pond. By piling brush in two long lines that came close together at one end, the antelope could be made to run through this narrow gap, so that many could be shot at close range. It was a good plan. Kimo had been with the Apaches once when they had killed many antelope with such a trap on the benches above Palo Duro Canyon, far to the east of the Rio Grande. But the difficulty was that the members of the Caiyaik Society would no longer follow Kimo or obey his commands.

Kimo had prayed to the mountain lion, his patron god, for

guidance. Twice the mountain lion had pictured for him two long lines of brush coming together at one end. Kimo dreamed of this trap. He dreamed, also, that many antelope would be killed and the Isleta people saved from starvation.

Kimo told of his dream to Pablo Abeyta. Pablo nodded his head. It was a good sign, a very good sign, he said. But the evil of the bear still sat upon the pueblo. There was one final ceremony by which the evil might be washed away. Pablo gave Kimo instructions on where to go and what to do.

Kimo, alone and in the full of the moon, walked west from the river to the edge of the Plains of St. Augustine. There, in the brush, he made a small camp, with no fire. Kimo caught a rabbit alive. It seemed to him that this half-grown jackrabbit came hopping up to him, unafraid. It was a good omen. Kimo dug a pit in an open place on the edge of the plain. The pit was deep enough to hide his body, with his head level with the ground. All of the dirt from the pit he carried in a blanket some distance away and hid carefully. Over the pit, he placed branches, leaves, and then grass. He left only a small opening near the middle. Near this opening, he tied the live rabbit by a thong attached to its leg.

For three days, Kimo crouched in the pit, waiting. During that time, he did not eat, nor did he have a fire, although the nights were bitter cold. On the third day, early in the morning, a golden eagle appeared in the sky. The bird circled. Its keen eye had seen the live rabbit hopping at the end of the thong. The eagle folded his wings and fell straight down toward the rabbit in a screaming dive. The talons of the bird closed over the rabbit's back. At the moment that the eagle struck, Kimo reached up through the hole and grabbed both the eagle's feet. He broke through the cover of poles and grass. The eagle, a large male, tore and flapped at Kimo's arm, ripping away furrows of skin and flesh. Deliberately, Kimo pulled out the long tail feathers and the longest of the wing feathers as the eagle struggled. When he had done this, he let the eagle go. The bird flopped away uncertainly, flying with difficulty. Kimo stanched the blood from his arms and returned to the pueblo.

That night in the kiva, Pablo Abeyta made twenty large prayer plumes from the eagle feathers. Each feather was tied by a thong to the top of a stick. The sticks were painted green and red—green for life and red for death. In the next full moon, Kimo carried the prayer sticks to the edge of the St. Augustine Plains and set them up in a long row in the ground. The ceremony was complete. The Eagle God of the air would overcome the black magic of the bear.

On the very next day, Kimo and the members of the Caiyaik Society began building the antelope trap. The Medicine Society, back at Isleta, held continuous ceremonials to be sure that no evil magic of any kind would interfere. By the end of the winter solstice, the trap was ready. The six war captains were enlisted to help with the hunt, especially since they had the only guns in the pueblo. Before they left for the hunt, the war captains fed cornmeal to the scalps of dead enemies kept in the kiva. This was to make sure that no spirit of a dead enemy would hinder the success of the antelope hunt.

Some men of the town, carrying blankets, were to act as drivers to harry the antelope into the open jaws of the trap. On the morning chosen, the winter sun was bright. There was little wind and only a little snow, which lay in patches in the shade of the scattered trees around the edge of the plain.

Kimo placed the bowmen and the war chiefs, with their Winchesters, on both sides of the trap behind the walls of brush. He checked to make certain that the men who carried the movable sections of juniper branches to close the mouth of the trap were well hidden and ready. Kimo signaled to the watchers on the far edge of the plain by waving a bright-colored headband. In the distance, the sunlight gleamed on another red band in answer. The line of men carrying blankets moved forward. In the center of the plain, the feeding antelope raised their heads.

The plan worked well. The Antelope Chief, the big buck with the wide-spreading horns, dashed forward to the front of the herds when the humans moved close, shouting and waving blankets. At full speed, the whole mass of animals moved across the plain and into the scattered trees on the far edge. The antelope often went that way. They were not afraid. The Chief Antelope led the whole herd straight toward the jaws of the trap. They were inside. Suddenly, he slid to a stop with all four feet braced. The other animals stopped. The whole herd stood in a huddled group. Ears twitched back and forth. The Chief Antelope looked first to one side, then to the other. He shook his head. He turned and bolted back through the other antelope. The whole herd turned and ran with him. Before a single arrow or shot could reach them, all the antelope were out of the jaws of the trap and into the open, running fast. Perhaps some flash of movement had caught their eye or the voice of the Bear God had warned them.

The hunters rose from their crouching positions behind the brush. They glared at Kimo. The evil magic still sat upon them. Behind Kimo, the antelope still ran. The Chief Antelope was far out in front.

Again, the Chief Antelope slid to a stop with the herd behind him. Just ahead of him was a flutter of motion. Twenty green and red sticks stood upright in the earth. The faint morning wind swung the eagle feathers that hung from their tips.

Snorting, the antelope wheeled together. Straight back through their own dust they came, as fast as they had gone. The Chief Antelope now ran with his mouth open and his tongue out. He seemed not to see the men as they scurried back behind the walls of brush and picked up their weapons. As fast as he could run, he galloped again through the wings of the trap and into the center. As the herd of antelope came into the narrow space between the lines of brush, Kimo again raised his hand. He jerked his arm down. Men ran forward carrying sections of brush before them. A shot boomed out. The Chief Antelope staggered but ran on. A ragged volley of shots thudded into the herd. Arrows arched through the air. The Chief Antelope fell to his knees and stopped. In panic, the other antelope turned and ran back. The men with the sections of brush before them had almost closed the gap between the wings of the trap. As they saw the moving men, the antelope doubled back along the walls of the trap. At point-blank range, the bowmen poured their arrows into the massed bodies. The Winchesters banged in a solid roar of shots. Antelope began to drop. Wounded animals hobbled and circled, trailing blood on the trampled ground. Through the dust and confusion, the bowmen sent arrow after arrow until their quivers were empty. Several of the hunters began to shout; they waved their bows above their heads. At this, the remnants of the herd turned and ran across the trap. Some of them jumped the brush wall at the far side. Others pushed straight through. A hunter at this spot was almost crushed by the stampede. The antelope poured through the gap in the wall and were gone.

Kimo and the other hunters entered the littered ground within the trap. They picked up fallen arrows and used them to kill wounded antelope. When the dust had settled, they counted three-times-twenty-and-seven animals. One of these was the Antelope Chief himself.

Men at Isleta still tell about the great antelope trap and the greatest kill of antelope that the Isleta hunters ever made. They tell, also, of Kimo, the Mountain Lion, the Chief of the Caiyaik Society, and the greatest hunter of them all. But the men of Isleta, hunters and farmers alike, will warn you of the powerful medicine of the bear, Chief of the Beast Gods.

WHITE MEDICINE BUFFALO

CHAPTER XVI

Blue Sky was sitting behind on the tailgate when it happened. His mother, Moon Hair, was riding among the heaped-up trade blankets and the camping things loaded on the wagon bed. The bull buffalo appeared out of nowhere, snorting and rumbling like thunder on a distant horizon. Crooked Hand, on the wagon box, saw the wedge-shaped back, so tall that it towered above him as he frantically jerked on the reins and whipped up the team. The shaggy head of the buffalo lowered as the hooked horns caught in the spokes of a front wheel. The bull twisted his massive neck and the whole wheel came away with the iron rim of the wagon tire fitting over his head like the wreath of a saint in the Spanish church.

Again the bull struck. This time he heaved beneath the edge of the wagon bed, sweeping his horns upward with a squealing grunt. The crash of splintering wood was mixed with the shrieks of the frightened horses. As the wagon tipped up and over, Moon Hair cried out once as she fell heavily under the hooves of the bull bison. Crooked Hand, too, was carried over with the impact. He tried to drag his ancient musket from beneath the wagon seat, but it never came clear. As Crooked Hand struggled half-erect from the wreckage around him, the bull turned quickly and gored him in the back. With short jerks of his ugly head, the bison drove one hooked horn between his shoulder blades. The old man stretched out his empty hand, as though to reach for the sky, then fell forward limply and lay on his face. The bison wrestled with his body for a moment, then trampled the scattered blankets where Moon Hair lay.

The two horses of the team broke loose as the kingpin came free. Still together in the traces, they galloped off, neighing and squealing, with the rope reins trailing behind. The bull bison turned toward the fleeing horses, so he did not see the boy who sprawled half-hidden by the upturned wagon. Blue Sky still clutched, in one small hand, a double-curved bow made from slabs of horn and bound with sinew. This was his most prized possession, all but forgotten in the middle of tragedy.

The boy watched with staring eyes as the bison loomed above him like a moving mountain. He saw that the animal was white on its hump, as though snow had fallen there. The bull trotted away, with anger still rumbling in his throat. Blue Sky crouched beneath the overturned wagon until darkness came and the coyotes began to talk to each other on the open plain. Other buffalo grazed past. Some snorted at the smell of blood and humans, but none came close.

As the moon rose over the edge of the prairie to look on the wreck of the wagon and the two figures that lay there, Blue Sky gathered blankets to cover the body of Crooked Hand, his father, and Moon Hair, his mother. The boy looked long at the face of each. He found that the features of the dead are not like the faces of the living, although they look the same.

They were not his real parents but foster folk. Blue Sky had been an orphan. His dead parents belonged to the Winter Black Eyes people of Isleta Pueblo in the Rio Grande Valley of New Mexico. It was usual for the Black Eyes Moiety to take care of its children, whatever their parentage. But Crooked Hand had been more that just a father. He had taught Blue Sky the ways of the hunt. He had brought him on this very trip, which had ended in bloody disaster. Most of all, Crooked Hand had given the lad a horn bow that even a strong hand could scarcely bend.

The slim lad that stood alone by the overturned wagon could not keep from whimpering. His widely spaced, dark eyes dimmed with unwanted moisture as he tried to compose the portly body of his mother in some dignified position. He turned Crooked Hand on his back so that the open mouth of the wound beneath his shoulder would be hidden. Crooked Hand's lips were open in almost a smile. He seemed ready to say something, although his body was beginning to stiffen. Blue Sky thought that his foster father wanted to tell him of the white buffalo. As the half-open lips remained silent, he covered the face with the edge of a blanket.

Blue Sky then took the flint and steel from the bag that hung at the waist of Crooked Hand. With this, he kindled a fire after much difficulty and clumsiness. He got out the cap-and-ball musket, saw to its priming as his father had taught him, and leaned it against the shattered wagon, close at hand. It mattered little that the musket was taller than the boy; he could scarcely have fired it, in any case.

So it was that on the next morning, a small boy started back toward the west along the wagon ruts that marked the trail to Isleta Pueblo in the Rio Grande Valley. He carried a horn bow in one hand and an enormous musket in the other. He did not look behind him as he left the remains of the wrecked wagon and the two blanket-covered bodies beside it. He thought only of a massive bull bison with a white-colored hump. He would know that animal among a thousand others of its kind.

The wagon, with its occupants, had come eastward five days to the Pecos River and three more days into the Great Plains. The Pueblo Indians often went on these forays into the eastern grasslands to hunt buffalo and bring back wagonloads of skins and dried meat. It was dangerous hunting, not so much because of the bison as because of the many other predatory Indians that ranged the open plains. There were Kiowas and Apaches, Utes and Comanches, too. Any one of these might kill a hunter to possess his musket or steal his horses. But of all the roving Indians, the Apaches were the worst. The Pueblo Indians called them Red Death, and the name was well deserved.

Crooked Hand had told Blue Sky of the Red Death. He had taught him how to read sign in faint moccasin tracks in the dusty trail. The Apaches seldom hunted buffalo themselves. In small raiding parties and mobile bands, they ranged the Pecos Valley, preying upon any whom they met. Small war parties made forays against the Pueblos. Seldom did they attack in a concerted manner with shouts and war cries. A silent arrow out of nowhere was usually the signal that the Apaches were present.

It was a sign such as this that told Blue Sky that death was behind him. On his second day's march after leaving the wagon, an arrow whispered past his cheek and buried half its length in the earth of the trail just ahead. He dropped his bow and swung the heavy musket around. The stock was so long that he could not fit it to his shoulder. Long before he had leveled the muzzle, a hand seized the barrel and wrenched the weapon from his grasp. Blue Sky looked directly into the face of an Apache warrior in full war paint.

He had heard no footfall, but then the Red Death always came silently. Fear paralyzed his limbs for only an instant. Crooked Hand had long ago told him that he who stands still through fear is soon dead. Blue Sky snatched the bow from the ground and reached across his shoulder to pull an arrow from his quiver. He fitted the neck to the string and raised the arrow level with the Apache's hideous face. The man himself carried a bow and a cluster of arrows in his hand, but he made no move to raise them or to unsling the buffalo hide shield that he carried on his back. Gravely, he watched Blue Sky as the lad struggled to bend the horn bow, but the diminutive muscles of the boy could not bring the tips back at all. The horn bow was as inert as a piece of stone. Finally, the Apache reached out one hand and took the bow, not ungently, from Blue Sky. There might have been a faint twinkle of amusement in the dark eyes of the Apache brave. Perhaps he had a boy of his own, and about the same size, in the Apache encampment on the bluff overlooking the Pecos River.

Before Blue Sky had an opportunity to run, the Apache seized him by one arm with a hand that closed like the talons of an eagle. The warrior led the tight-lipped lad away from the wagon-rutted trail and into the breaks and mesas of the Pecos country. Blue Sky was to live in that wild area for the next five years.

It was not the custom of the Apaches to kill young captives that they might take alive. Instead, they made them part of their own people, to replace children that had died or to make happy some couple that the gods had left childless. Blue Sky came, in this way, to the family of an aged warrior whose two sons had been killed in battle with the Spanish soldiers in the Estancia Valley. Blue Sky might delight his declining years and might also become a great warrior with his teaching.

Blue Sky was allowed to keep his horn bow and have some freedom in the Apache camp. As his muscles grew stronger with the passing months, he learned to bend the unresilient horn and to shoot accurately. Often, he oiled the bow with bear fat to keep the sinews firm and the horn alive. By the time Blue Sky had passed as many winters as the fingers on three hands, he could bend the bow as easily as a wooden one, but the arrows that he shot went twice as far as any shafts from a common bow. The Apaches of the encampment had few guns. Such a bow as Blue Sky possessed was a great asset to a warrior on a raiding party. But Blue Sky found no pleasure in plundering the Spanish settlements around Santa Fe. He did join with several forays against the wagon trains that came across the upper prairies to the Raton Pass. He fought also in several skirmishes with the Utes along the Canadian River. During these times, he learned to ride and care for a horse.

The Apaches taught him to shoot with his horn bow from the back of an animal at a full gallop. He could hang by his heels and shoot beneath the horse's neck while keeping the animal's body between himself and an enemy bowman. Blue Sky was accomplished in all these things, far better than any of the young Apaches with whom he rode. Nonetheless, he was a bitter disappointment to his foster parents in the Apache band. He would not take an Apache girl for his mate, nor would he collect scalps from the fallen enemy as any Apache warrior should.

As Blue Sky approached full manhood, he turned more and more to the hunting of animals for meat and less to raiding against other humans for scalps and glory. It was his horn bow and his broad-bladed arrows that brought down antelope that fed the encampment. During these hunting trips, he had visited Isleta Pueblo only once. The people there feared him in his Apache dress, although his round face was that of a Rio Grande Indian and he spoke the Tiwa tongue. Even the dogs in the pueblo barked and yelped at the unfamiliar scent of his Apache leggings, so that he could not dismount in the place. No one seemed to remember the slim lad who had ridden away on a buffalo hunt so many years before.

Among the Apaches, also, he was a stranger. He found no profit in their war parties and never joined in the Apache dances to celebrate victory. Blue Sky hunted alone and camped alone. The other Apaches wisely let him go his way, believing that Blue Sky was a man possessed by a spirit.

On every hunting trip to the east, Blue Sky rode past the place where the weathered timber of Crooked Hand's wagon still protruded from the rank grama grass sod. He had buried Crooked Hand and Moon Hair in the Apache manner, collecting their bones and tying them in bundles of buckskin. Blue Sky hung these packages by thongs to the branches of a cottonwood tree in a small creek bottom some distance from the wreck of the wagon.

He rode over to inspect the place and make sure that the wolves had not pulled the bundles down. The shapeless burial shrouds were, as always, swinging in the prairie wind. But this day, in the shade beneath the tree, there stood a buffalo bull. The animal was white as snow all over his back, and the hair on his head was the color of dirty alkali.

Blue Sky sat immobile on his horse. This bull that stood so

quietly with closed eyes was a trick of the spirits. The white buffalo had returned as a ghost to haunt the place where Crooked Hand and Moon Hair had been killed.

The bull slowly shifted his feet and flicked his dusty flank with a swinging tail. At the movement, Blue Sky's horse started violently. The animal had not noticed the buffalo before. Now he reared and squealed at the close smell of the bull. Blue Sky pulled an arrow from the quiver behind his shoulder. As he fitted the nock to the string, the horse reared again. Blue Sky clutched at the matted hair of the mane with one hand. The arrow slipped from his fingers. The terrified pony dropped his head between outstretched forelegs and pitched suddenly forward. Blue Sky clung to the arched back of the swinging horse, but he had dropped his horn bow. Again, the pony pitched forward and came down hard on braced legs. At the jar of the impact, Blue Sky fell sideways. His hand still held a tuft of hair from the horse's mane. The arrows slipped from his quiver as he rolled beneath the very feet of the medicine buffalo.

Blue Sky watched his horse buck away and stand, panting. The jar of the fall had dazed him. He looked around for his horn bow. At the same time, he hunched his shoulders for the charge of the bull buffalo from behind. In another instant, those hooked horns would tear into his back, as they had his father's. Blue Sky crawled forward. There was the bow among the leaves on the ground. One loose arrow lay not far to the side. He grasped the bow with an uncertain hand. The arrow was partly splintered and one feather was gone. He fitted it to the string. Still on his knees, he turned to face the buffalo charge. There was the cottonwood tree, as before, with the burial bundles swinging from the first limb. The white bull had vanished.

From that day, Blue Sky hunted for the medicine buffalo. He camped near the burial tree and waited for the bull. There were scattered herds of bison that fed over the adjacent prairies. All these he examined for the white bull that might be among them. It was spring, and the buffalo were on the move to the northern hunting grounds. As the animals fed past or moved slowly north in long lines, Blue Sky rode among them with his bow ready. Of the thousands of bison that he saw, there was no one that had a back the color of new snow. At the end of a summer of lonely wandering and watching, he returned to the Mescalera Apache camp on the Pecos River.

It was here that his foster father, with a solemn face and sad eyes, received him and told a story that had come to the Apache band during the summer. Across the Plains, the word was passed from tribe to tribe that a white medicine buffalo had appeared in the country of the Wichitas, to the east. The hunters who had brought in the story did not know whether this might be the same rogue bull that had ravaged the Canadian River country. Such were the movements of the bison herd that it might be the same animal carrying its medicine and destruction to a new place.

It was characteristic of Blue Sky that he asked no one's advice. That same evening, he set out alone for the country of the Wichitas. He carried no gun, although he might have procured a Spanish musket, since these were becoming more common in the Pecos country. Blue Sky relied on the power of his horn bow. He rode an Apache pony and led another horse behind, loaded lightly with a Spanish pack saddle and a rawhide sack of provisions, and he packed a parfleche, after the manner of the Plains tribes.

But Blue Sky was no Plainsman. His long black hair was caught up at the back of his head in a bulky bun tied with a piece of red trade cloth. His placid face, old far beyond his years, was the face of a pueblo man with a purpose. Even though Blue Sky wore the clout and leggings of a Mescalero Apache, it was obvious to any who might see him that he was one of the pueblo people and out of place in the buffalo country.

It was for this reason that Blue Sky rode at night and picketed his horses in hidden, wooded canyons during the daylight hours. It was late summer when he had started on the quest for the white buffalo of the Wichitas, but the flowers had already faded from the prairie before Blue Sky reached the lower Canadian and the hunting grounds of the Wichitas.

A band of buffalo hunters of the Wichita tribe were camped in a wooded bottom near a stream. Although there were twenty lodges at this place and sentries guarded every approach to the camp, a single man appeared in their midst at the edge of the fire. Before the Wichita could jump to their feet and grasp their weapons, the stranger raised his hand and swept it palm outward away from his breast in the token of friendship.

"I come to the country of the Wichitas seeking a medicine buffalo, a bull, white as the snow of the winter." Blue Sky spoke in the language of the Apaches.

None of the hunters gathered around the fire answered or gave any sign that he understood. Even the women and the children who came from the lodges to see the curious stranger made no answer.

Blue Sky spoke again, using the universal sign language by which all the Plains tribes could communicate with each other. Several of the men nodded solemnly and pointed to the north.

"We have seen such a white buffalo," they answered. A hunting chief stood up and advanced toward Blue Sky. Touching his eyes and the thighs of his legs, he explained that they had seen a buffalo as white as snow but had not killed him. Blue Sky stood silently for several minutes as he heard the news. With no word of farewell, he turned and stepped back into the shadows of the trees. No one heard his footsteps as he left and no dog barked at his going.

Blue Sky knew that the country to the north was the domain of the Pawnee. So fierce were the Pawnee war parties that their reputations had reached even to the Rio Grande. And yet he did not hesitate, even though he knew that his curious, bound-up hair would make a valuable trophy for some Pawnee brave lucky enough to kill him.

During the fall, the buffalo herds fed in small groups. It was not yet the time when the bison gathered in herds for their winter migration. Although it was easier to hunt them in the smaller groups, the meat was less desirable. The cows were thin with their milking calves. The bulls had not yet acquired their winter layer of fat.

Blue Sky searched from sunrise to sunset among such groups of feeding buffalo as he could find. He scanned every herd. As he saw that each animal was dark in color in the distance, he rode on to the next valley or the next low rise to look at others. He ignored the fact that each day he exposed himself to some war party that might have found and followed his horse tracks. Blue Sky seldom stopped to rest and took no time to dry buffalo meat to refill his parfleche.

Late autumn became winter as Blue Sky systematically covered the shallow river valleys and the rolling undulations of the Great Plains. His dark eyes had looked at thousands of shaggy bison, but not one of these had the light coat or even the suggestion of whiteness for which he was seeking. Other herds of buffalo began to straggle from the north and drift to the south country as snow fell on the upper plains. The animals gathered together in masses so huge that the eye of a single man could not see across such a herd as they moved. At such times, it was dangerous for even a large hunting party to go among these animals. For a single man, it was to ask for death.

Like a man demented, Blue Sky rode his horse among the herds. Often, he would stop his mount and stand at full height on its back to look out over the moving bison in the distance. Never once did he see an animal that was white. When the snow flurries came down over the prairies, it was more difficult to single out a white buffalo in the midst of so much whiteness. Still, Blue Sky rode on as the bison herds moved southward.

In this way, Blue Sky searched through the swales and river bottoms of what is now western Kansas. In one such river bottom, he stopped his thin horse behind a cutbank in crusted snow that reached up to the middle of the animal's legs. Below, in the brush and stunted cottonwoods along the creek, was a scattered herd of cow bison gathered to keep out of the wind as the main migration of buffalo moved on to the south. These cows were thin and obviously old. Most of them would never see the grass freshen in the spring in that valley. Days before, Blue Sky had eaten the last jerked meat in his parfleche. Even a stringy cow would be food. Here in the sheltered creek valley, there was little danger of a stampede.

Taking his bow from his shoulder, Blue Sky warmed the cold horn between his hands so that it would not crack. As he walked through the crusted snow toward the creek, a mangy bison looked at him with dull eyes but made no move to run. Blue Sky advanced to within a few paces of the beast and fitted an arrow to the string. He walked to one side to make a killing shot behind the shoulder. Still, the cow stood with head held low and dark eyes blank with the apathy of age and near death. Blue Sky drew the bow slowly back and sank upon one knee in the snow.

A whinny sounded shrilly in the quiet of the creek bottom. Blue Sky glanced over his shoulder. His horse was looking upward, with both ears pointed toward the high bank above. A single, small tree was outlined darkly against the mat of white at the edge of the valley. There was no other living thing in sight.

Suddenly, beside the tree, a horseman appeared, as if by magic from the snow. The man carried a long lance with a scalp fixed below its point. His own hair was cut in a crested roach that made him look taller than he was. Another man rode up beside the first—and then another. All of them had the crested headdress and face paint like the first.

Pawnees! The fiercest of all the Plains tribes. Every hunter on the Plains,—Dakotas, Cheyennes, Arapahoes, Crows, Osages, and even the warlike Comanches—feared the Pawnees and avoided their hunting grounds.

A group of seven Pawnees now sat their horses in an uneven line with their leader. Their mounts were breathing hard, and puffs of white vapor stood out before their nostrils in the cold air. The Pawnees were on a winter hunting party, as their lances indicated, but such a hunting party could just as well collect the long-haired scalp of this stranger who knelt in the snow by the creek.

The first Pawnee was an older man. From the scalp on his lance, it was evident that he had already counted coup on a human enemy and was the hunt leader of this group. The young warriors at his side reared their horses in impatience. The old Pawnee looked carefully up and down the valley. Only a few scattered bison showed at the edges of the willows. Certainly, no other human was close or the buffalo would be more restless.

In the crusted snow, this curious stranger with the long hair could not escape. Nor could he reach his horse in time. A lance would spit him like a rabbit as he turned to run.

The Pawnee leader suddenly flailed the flanks of his horse with his moccasined heels. The animal started on a plunging run down the side of the little valley. The other warriors raised the scalping cry and strung out in a line after their leader. The old Pawnee in front lowered his lance so that the butt rested beneath his elbow. The point was of iron—the result of some raid against the white settlements in the Missouri Valley. With such a lance, a skilled horseman could pierce a buffalo with a single thrust or kill a man even through a shield.

Blue Sky had no shield, nor could he dodge or run in the crusted snow, but he did not think of escaping, in any case. He saw that the

Pawnees would have to swing to one side to avoid the cutbank where his own mount was tethered. As Blue Sky still knelt in the snow, he drew all the arrows from his quiver and stuck them upright in the crust before him with their feathered butts just below his hand.

The old Pawnee warrior rounded the cutbank and turned his horse toward Blue Sky, across the level floor of the valley. He was almost close enough for Blue Sky to see the streaks of yellow on his face. The point of the lance was a blur before him. The other warriors galloped their horses in a line through the broken trail in the snow left by the leader.

Blue Sky took aim past the neck of the Pawnee's horse. As he bent the horn bow and released the arrow, it seemed one motion. There was a sodden thud and a gasp as the blow of the shaft knocked the breath from the lungs of the Pawnee. He clutched, with curled fingers, at the feathers on his chest. Before his body had toppled backward from his horse, Blue Sky had snatched another arrow from the snow and again bent the horn bow. The second arrow struck the next Pawnee in the ribs below the shoulder. He dropped his lance and sagged sideways from his horse.

The savage onslaught caught the Pawnees unprepared. Horses jostled each other and milled in the snow. Another arrow leapt from the horn bow and buried itself to the feathers in the throat of another warrior.

The others frantically jerked on rawhide reins to turn their mounts. In a group, they galloped back up the side of the valley. As they ran, another arrow followed faster than the swiftest horse. The shaft struck the thigh of the last warrior and glanced along the bone so that the head stuck out before his leg. The man grasped the arrow in one hand to pull it out and urged on his laboring horse with the other.

Above, on the crest of the slope, the Pawnees slowed and turned their mounts. The wounded man had broken the arrow in his leg and pulled out the fragments. Tight-lipped to choke back the cries of pain that no Pawnee may utter, the man gripped his thigh to hold back the spurts of blood that pumped between his fingers. The remaining Pawnees talked among themselves and looked often down at the solitary figure of Blue Sky, who still knelt in the snow with a row of arrows upright before him.

A single Pawnee, perhaps the youngest of the group, unslung a bow from behind his shoulder and handed his lance to the man beside him. The young warrior talked excitedly and in boastful tones. A lone man sitting in the snow—could such a stranger stop a real Pawnee bowman? As he rode downward through the trampled snow, he guided his mount on a slanting course toward Blue Sky so as to gallop in front of him at close range.

As he rode within arrow shot, the Pawnee dropped to the far side of his horse and clung there with legs and heels so that he could shoot beneath the horse's neck. Blue Sky had used this very trick on a dozen occasions when he rode with the Apaches. An enemy had no target except a leg above the horse's back and a hand and arm holding a bow beneath the neck. No bowman could hit such a difficult mark.

The Pawnee was already close. He gave the scalping yell and bent his bow. The stationary figure of Blue Sky was an easy target.

Blue Sky held his bow ready but made no move to shoot. Still, his face was calm as the horse raced past him throwing up clumps of snow from its hooves. In that instant, Blue Sky raised his bow and bent the tips back as far as his straining muscles could pull the stiff horn. The snap of the bowstring and the solid clump of the arrow striking flesh were one sound. The shaft struck the neck of the running horse and passed on through to pierce the man on the other side. The Pawnee dropped his bow but clung to the moving horse for an instant. Then he dropped away like a spider by the flame of a fire. The arrow had entered his chest, and there was blood on the snow where he fell. The horse, too, collapsed just beyond and lay quivering.

Above, on the edge of the valley, the three Pawnees slowly rode away. Only two of them lived to reach their camp to the eastward. The story they told was of a madman with long hair. This stranger shot a bow of light, and his arrows were lightning that killed, even through the body of a horse.

In midwinter of that same year, Blue Sky walked into a Cheyenne encampment. He led a horse covered with mud and limping in one forefoot. Blue Sky's Apache moccasins were frayed and without soles to protect his feet from the frozen ground. He wore no buffalo robe to shield his bare shoulders from the biting wind. He did not seem to feel the cold but walked erect, staring straight ahead as the people gathered around to see the scarecrow of a man with dark eyes like an eagle.

The Cheyenne chief was amazed when the stranger questioned him about a certain white buffalo even before he would take food. But the Cheyenne had seen no white medicine buffalo. They had heard that such a buffalo was in the country of the Arapahoes to the north. He was a great beast, a bull, with a pure white hump. The story had been told that this white bull had galloped through an Arapahoe encampment. He had gored two warriors and then tossed a whole lodge on his horns, to disappear before a single arrow could reach him.

Blue Sky's eyes gleamed with intensity as the Cheyenne chief finished in pantomime the telling of the story of the white buffalo bull. Only then did Blue Sky eat sparingly of cooked buffalo paunch mixed with berries. The Cheyenne gave him a fresh horse and dried meat to take with him. Blue Sky left that same night with new soles on his moccasins and new hope in his heart.

But Blue Sky did not find the white medicine buffalo in the

country of the Arapahoes. The bison herds had moved again, and the white bull had disappeared from the grassland of the prairie.

In this next year, Blue Sky appeared in many encampments of many tribes. Most of them had already heard of the solitary Pueblo Indian who roamed the Plains looking for a white medicine buffalo. It was told around the campfires of the buffalo hunters that this was no ordinary human. Neither he nor his horse left any tracks behind him. He appeared suddenly in the midst of an encampment, asking always for a white medicine buffalo. Then, he would disappear as mysteriously as he had come. Also, he could cover great distances in a single night—and never slept. The hunters told of the season when this mysterious stranger had sought the white buffalo in the hunting grounds of the Cheyennes and was seen at almost the same time in the country of the Arapahoes, many days travel to the north. Others told of seeing his figure sitting erect on his dark-colored horse on moonlit nights. He rode fearlessly among herds of bison that would stampede any ordinary mortal.

Blue Sky's reputation among all the Plains tribes was heightened when the white medicine touched him. In the third year of his quest, his dark hair turned iron gray and then pure white. His face, also, had set in lines of radiating wrinkles of a man twice his age. His body bowed forward at the shoulders, and the hands that still clutched the horn bow were gnarled and weather-beaten. These changes might have come about because of the intensity of the search or because Blue Sky seldom slept, either by day or by night. Although many daughters of great chiefs, from many tribes, had been offered to the great medicine man, he took no wife and, indeed, looked upon no woman except to thank her gravely for any food that she might offer.

Although the memory of his foster parents, Crooked Hand and Moon Hair, had grown dim with the passing years, Blue Sky returned periodically to the place of their death. Long ago, the rank prairie grass had grown up around the weathered remnants of the wrecked wagon. Only one great wheel, protected by its iron tire, protruded above the tangle. Yet in this place, Blue Sky felt that he was closest to his goal. Here again, the white medicine buffalo might come out of nowhere and appear before him.

As he sat his horse and quietly looked down at the place, as he had so many times before, he noticed that some other passing people had left prayer plumes, tipped with eagle feathers, on the spot. It was good, Blue Sky thought to himself, that the Isleta hunters, as they passed that way, might remember Crooked Hand and the white medicine buffalo.

Blue Sky turned his head quickly as he heard the rapid hoofbeats of an approaching horse. It was a single warrior, an Apache by the looks of his leggings. Blue Sky sat stolidly until the warrior galloped up and stopped his horse with braced legs.

"We have sought you many moons and hoped you would come to this place, Blue Sky. We have seen the white buffalo."

Blue Sky leaned forward intently, as though to suck this information from the man. The Apache warrior quickly told how a white bull buffalo had gored a horse and killed its rider only weeks before.

"Four days' journey to the east by the forks of the river that flows from the mountains." Blue Sky had already turned his horse to the east as the man was speaking. "The Kiowas make war on all Apaches."

Blue Sky did not wait to hear the end of his words but rode swiftly toward the east. By sunset of the second day, he had covered what was ordinarily a four-day journey. As he reached the forks of the great river, he saw the smoke of the Kiowa encampment in the distance.

On the next morning, he found a fresh buffalo carcass and the marks of travois poles where squaws had skinned the animal and carried off the meat. There were prints of unshod horses' hooves amount the bison trails that crisscrossed the grasslands. Blue Sky saw smoke signals in the distance where a hunting party gave the sign that they had made a kill and called for the women to pack in the meat.

It was that same afternoon, as he circled wide to avoid the Kiowa encampment, that he found the great herd of bison. The animals were restless, since the Kiowas had already made several drives to cut out the younger animals. The big herd bulls roared and bellowed in the distance as they circled warily on the outskirts of the main mass of cows and young. Even in the setting sun, Blue Sky imagined he saw a single bull bison in the distance that was lighter in color than the rest. Even though the animal was a mile away, and in the middle of a milling mass of his kind, Blue Sky thought he saw clearly the massive triangular head with the hooked horns on either side.

He slept without a fire in a small hollow on the edge of a mesa. He tethered his horse close so that the animal could not graze away and attract the attention of the Kiowas. At daybreak, he climbed to the edge of the mesa and looked to the north.

As the morning light grew stronger, he saw in the distance the dark cloud shadow of the herd. The animals had scattered to graze as the sun warmed them. Some of the cows were lying down with their calves, but even these were watchful. The herd bulls still grumbled along the fringes of the slowly moving mass.

Over the shifting silhouettes of dark bodies was a dimness that was partly morning mist and party dust stirred by trailing hooves. Only in one spot could Blue Sky see light against the dark. And there it was! A white hump moving among the others. Perhaps some bull with caked mud on his coat from rolling in a wallow. No. There it showed again, as the animals moved. This one back was white as no mud could be. There was the wedged hump and the white head. White as though snow had fallen there!

Blue Sky's eyes narrowed, and his hands clenched. There could be no doubt. It was the medicine bull! Suddenly he felt tired. The drive that had bolstered him through so many sleepless nights was gone. His muscles sagged. A burning behind his eyes blotted out the form of the white buffalo in the distance.

With fumbling hands, he opened the parfleche that he carried and took from it a bag containing his most powerful medicine. There was the tip of an arrow that had killed a grizzly bear and, therefore, possessed great power. In another small bundle in the parfleche, Blue Sky carried a solid lead musket ball that his father had given him. The medicine of the musket ball brought the protection of his foster father close. Because this was the crucial time, Blue Sky prayed aloud to the rising sun, holding these powerful talismans in his hands. He said simply, "Give me, O Great Spirit, the strength to bend my bow. Let my arrow find the heart of the medicine buffalo."

It was impossible for a single man, even though wellmounted on a hardy horse, to stalk buffalo in a large herd. The animals, already skittish after being hunted by the Kiowas, would stampede at the slightest provocation. Anyone, whether on foot or on horseback, would be quickly swept to destruction by such a racing sea of hooves and horns as that of this unpredictable herd.

Blue Sky knew these things and knew how small his chances were of cutting out a single animal, even from the edge of the herd. Although strengthened by his own medicine, yet he stumbled as he descended the mesa. He removed the folded blanket that was strapped to the back of his horse as a saddle. The bridle, also, might have too much man-scent upon it. Blue Sky substituted a short piece of rawhide, which he twisted around his horse's lower jaw. Blue Sky's hands were sweaty as he slid belly-down upon his horse with his horn bow in his hand. Three arrows only he carried in his teeth. He left his quiver and his parfleche by the foot of the mesa.

Blue Sky rode his horse slowly and diagonally toward the bison. As he dropped down into a hollow just out of arrow range from the nearest bulls, he was momentarily out of sight. Many bison had been there the night before. Blue Sky slipped from his horse and, still holding the reins, picked up several handfuls of mud and buffalo chips and rubbed them over the horse's back and legs. Then he also covered himself with the same materials. It was only in this way that the horse's smell and his own scent might be deadened somewhat to the sensitive nostrils of the bison.

When he rode out of the small hollow again and into full view of the nearest bulls, Blue Sky was not sitting erect. He lay at full length along the horse's back, speaking softly into the animal's ear to ease his nervousness at the nearness of the bison. Blue Sky allowed his horse to wander and even to graze a little as he came close to the first buffalo. The nearest bull rumbled in his throat and raised his head suspiciously but did not charge. Blue Sky moved his hand slowly on the rope reins as he guided his pony in among the bison. If the horse whinnied once or shied violently at one of the bulls, he was lost.

With the smell and noise of buffalo all around, the horse grew more nervous and showed a tendency to bolt. Still, Blue Sky soothed the animal with words and by a soft touch on the rawhide reins. He walked his horse between the scattered groups of buffalo, working ever closer toward the center of the mass where he had marked out the white back of the medicine bull.

It was a barren cow, ill at ease, perhaps, because she had no calf that year, that started the stampede. Blue Sky saw the cow to one side. She stared curiously at him and the horse, wriggling her nose as she smelled intently the strange combination. Some whiff of horse or human scent must have come to her nostrils. She trotted forward and smelled again to make sure. Blue Sky could see her shaggy face and wicked dark eyes so close that he might have reached out the tip of his bow and whipped her across her snout. The cow buffalo roared in fright. Her tail stiffened and stood straight up. She pivoted suddenly. Blue Sky's horse shied away, crying shrilly in fear. All around, other buffalo raised their tails in fright and sensed the danger. Others that could not see or smell the man and the horse in their midst milled and circled with heads erect. The scent of fear was in the air. Without direction, the herd began to move. The rumble of hooves became a roar, and the roar an avalanche of sound. Bison bodies pressed close. Massive heads moved up and down in the rhythm of running.

Blue Sky leaned forward and pulled frantically on the rawhide to jerk the horse's head around. The panicky animal reared and sidled. The very weight of the bison on both sides hemmed in the horse, and he turned with the pressure of jostling bodies. The whole mass, with the horse and man in the middle, began to run without reason toward the west.

As Blue Sky looked out over the solid mass of backs, he could scarcely see the edges of the herd through the rising dust. There was no escape. The moving bison were running all in the same direction now, their bodies pressing close together. Soon, one of those hooked horns would disembowel his horse. Then horse and rider, together, would go down to be beaten into the bloody dust beneath those thousands of hooves.

As Blue Sky looked for some opening, some place where the rising and falling backs of the buffalo were not so close together, he saw a white hump through the dust. The medicine bull was only a few animals away and almost parallel with him. Blue Sky leaned over and whipped the nearest buffalo savagely across the eyes and snout with the back of his bow. The terrified animal reared back and made a small opening. Blue Sky turned his horse's head and kicked the animal into the gap. The buffalo's horn swept along the horse's haunch, leaving a red streak, but the horse did not fall.

Blue Sky kicked and beat at the next bison and crowded against it with his horse's flank. He gained another place. Only one more bull separated him from the white buffalo. This bull twitched his head sideways and rolled his eyes whenever the horse moved close.

Blue Sky picked an arrow from between his teeth and fitted the nock to the string on the horn bow. He bent the bow with a quick backward motion of his arm and leaned low beside the bull. He loosed the string and the arrow buried itself to the feathers in the chest of the bison. The bull roared but kept on running. In a moment, blood appeared in the animal's nostrils and his front legs began to falter. As the bull went to his knees, Blue Sky pressed in front and his horse ran alongside the white medicine buffalo.

The animal seemed not to notice him but ran silently. Blue Sky saw that the shaggy head, even the legs, of the bison were a dirty white. He felt an aura, too, of power that radiated from the animal. For some time, as his horse ran steadily, he stared open-mouthed at the bison beside him. But at any moment, if his horse should step into a prairie dog hole or the other bison close in around him, the opportunity would be lost.

Blue Sky took another arrow from his mouth. As he galloped, he glanced along the shaft to see if it had warped. He fitted it to the string and bent the bow back. Never had the horn bow been under such a strain. He waited an instant until the galloping of his own horse and the rise and fall of the running buffalo were together. He leaned low and shot. The arrow disappeared into the white flank of the bison and dropped out on the other side. But the medicine buffalo galloped on as before.

Blue Sky drew his last arrow and bent the bow until the tips almost touched his shoulder and arm on either side. He aimed forward for the rib cage of the bison, although here the arrow might hit a bone and the point be deflected. As he released the string, he saw the puff of dust from the shaggy coat of the bison as the broad flint tip bit home. The shaft sank its whole length behind the shoulder of the beast.

Still, the buffalo ran steadily on. For the first time, Blue Sky felt fear as well as awe. Such a medicine buffalo could not be killed by an ordinary arrow. As the dust clouds of the stampede boiled around him, Blue Sky looked up and asked the Great Spirit for guidance. In that instant, the white buffalo crumpled all at once and fell forward.

Blue Sky jerked his horse to a sliding stop and pitched off in front of the white buffalo. He scarcely noticed as the snorting animals on either side swept the pony away and left him standing in a sea of grinding hooves and clashing horns. His eyes were fixed on the wedge-shaped hump with hair as white as his own. Could this be the same medicine bull after so many years? Or were such spirits immortal? As if in answer, the buffalo opened its eyes. They were as pink as the sunset and seemed to glow brightly, like two embers fanned by the wind. The eyes closed; the great body shuddered and fell over on its side.

Blue Sky dropped the horn bow from his hand and stepped forward reverently. Reaching out, he touched the head of the bull. The power of the medicine coursed up his arm and filled his whole being. In that instant, he sat on the wagon box again with Crooked Hand beside him, and his mother, Moon Hair, was there, too. A great bull buffalo, with a hump as white as snow, appeared out of nowhere, with a growl like distant thunder. The emaciated form of Blue Sky fell forward as the last of the frantic bison herd closed over the spot.

The Kiowas found them together, there in the trampled earth, after the stampede had passed. Blue Sky lay as though asleep, with his hand on the head of the white buffalo. He died that night, although there seemed to be no mark upon his thin body that might have caused death. The hunters of the Plains know that the medicine of the white buffalo is more deadly than an arrow.

The Kiowas buried the white-haired stranger and the white buffalo together, placing the two bodies on a platform built of cottonwood limbs. Such a white buffalo was worth a hundred ponies or twenty beautiful wives, but there was no Kiowa there who would claim such a treasure. Each man that had a part in the burial handled the bodies with long poles so that the medicine would not come close. Even the horn bow was placed reverently on top of the grave by the Kiowa medicine man himself, who spent three days afterward in cleansing his hand from the touch of it.

These many years since the burial, the place in the Kiowa country has been called White Buffalo. It is here that a Pueblo wanderer, far from his native Rio Grande, sleeps beside the bones of a great bull bison. Any man, if he is near this spot, can feel the power of the medicine that still radiates from the ground near a pile of scattered bones and rotted cottonwood limbs. Such a man's hair may turn white or his skin be blotched with sudden pallor. This is the power of the White Medicine Buffalo.